CSM® (CERTIFIED SCRUMMASTER) EXAM PRACTICE QUESTIONS

HOW TO PASS CSM® (CERTIFIED SCRUMMASTER) IN 2 WEEKS

THIYAGARAJAN PERUMAL
MBA, PMP, PMI-ACP, CSM, ITIL, 6 Sigma Black Belt

---

www.Projectmgtcoach.com

CSM® (CERTIFIED SCRUMMASTER) EXAM PRACTICE QUESTIONS
HOW TO PASS CSM® (CERTIFIED SCRUMMASTER) IN 2 WEEKS

Table of Contents

About the CSM Exams

- A certified scrum master helps the project teams to use the Scrum process and the results in overall project successes. CSM's understands Scrum values, it practices and provides a level of knowledge and expertise for the success of the project.
- The candidate must attend a two-day Certified Scrum Master Course, the final step in becoming a Scrum Master (CSM) in Scrum is successfully passing the online CSM examination.

Plan on taking about an hour to complete the CSM exam, but you don't need to finish the exam in one session. You can stop and restart as many times as needed. You can also skip, go back and bookmark some questions for later review. Review your bookmarked questions before submitting your test for scoring. If you don't pass your test, you can take it a second time at no cost. The Scrum Alliance charges small fees for each subsequent attempt after the second.

- If you don't pass the test you will be shown the questions that you missed but it won't tell you the right answer. So you need to research the right answer.
- If you don't pass the test, then you can take it as a second time as free of cost, but you need to

take it within 90 days of your CSM class. After that Scrum Alliance will charge $25 for each subsequent attempt.

Can I become CSM without attending the class for CSM?

- No. You must attend the class from the provider or their recognized REP's.

What is the membership fee?

- Certified Scrum Trainers pay the initial membership fee for every student who completes the Scrum master course. This membership fee covers the cost of a CSM exam and the first two years of membership.

Where can I find the link to take CSM examination?

- After finishing your CSM course, you'll receive an email from Scrum Alliance that includes a link to create your login credentials. The first step will be to take the test. Once the test is complete you will be asked to accept a license agreement and setup your online profile. It could take up to two weeks after course completion to receive your welcome mail.

- Once the test is complete you will be asked to accept a license agreement and your CSM badge will appear on your profile.

What can I expect from the CSM exam?

- The test consists of a mixture of multiple-choice questions. It will take about 60 minutes to finish it. You'll be required to demonstrate your understanding of key Scrum elements including but not limited to, General Scrum knowledge, Scrum roles, Scrum artifacts, and Scrum meetings.

What is the cost of the CSM exam?

- The cost of the test is included in the cost of the CSM course and which is paid by your trainer. There will be two free attempts paid and it will be done by the trainer, but after that, each subsequent attempt will cost you $25.

How soon after my course do I have to complete the CSM exam?

- After receiving your membership email, you will have 90 days to take and complete the test.

What are the benefits of Certified Scrum Master Certification?

- Develop your carrier opportunity by staying relevant and marketable across all industry sectors which are following agile practices.
- Demonstrate to employers and colleagues your attainment of core Scrum knowledge.
- With your CSM certificate, you can join the local user groups, online social networks, and additional resources that are only available to Scrum Alliance members.

How long do I need to wait for the results of the CSM examination?

- The results are declared immediately; you will come to know after submitting the exam online.

CSM REQUIREMENTS

- Attend a live online or in-person course taught by a Certified Scrum Trainer® (CST®), or receive private coaching from a Certified Agile Coach (CAC).
- After successfully completing the course, you will need to accept the License Agreement, take the 50 question CSM test, and answer 37 out of the 50 questions correctly within the 60-minute time limit.
- The passing score is 74%. You will not be able to pause the test, but questions can be bookmarked to answer later during the 60-minute time limit. For more information about which types of topics and questions are included on the CSM test, please refer to our CSM Test Specifications Outline.
- After receiving the initial welcome email from Scrum Alliance that contains the account activation link, you will have 90 days to complete the CSM test for free. Students are also given two free attempts to pass the CSM test. But if you fail the test twice or complete it after 90 days, you will have to pay $25 USD test attempt fee

How do I take the CSM test?

- In order to access the CSM test, you must first take an in-person two day (16 hours) or live online (14 hours) Certified Scrum Master® course with one of our Certified Scrum Trainers (CSTs®.) Course attendance is required to earn the CSM certification; individuals cannot skip the training required to gain access to the online CSM test. Please visit our Course Search page to find a CSM course near you.

- After completing the Certified Scrum Master course, you will receive a welcome email including a link to activate your Scrum Alliance® certification account where you will be able to complete the CSM test.

To take your test, please go to our website
- https://www.scrumalliance.org/login

1. Sign in with your login credentials (Note: Your registered email address and username is included in the "Welcome CSM" email)
2. Hover over Hello, [Your Name] in the top right-hand corner and select My Dashboard
3. Click on "Take CSM test"
4. Select your language and continue
5. You will be redirected to the test.com site where you will be presented with the exam.
6. Please make sure to turn OFF your pop-up blockers before you begin the test.

If you haven't received the welcome email to activate your certification account:

- ✓ Ensure the email was not directed to your inbox's spam/junk folder.
- ✓ Use the email address that you provided to your instructor when you attended the in-person course.
- ✓ Send a support ticket to support@scrumalliance.org with the date, location, and instructor's name of the CSM course that you attended.

Can I take the CSM® test without attending an in-person Certified Scrum Master® course?

- Those who want to earn a Certified Scrum Master® (CSM®) certification are required to take either an in-person, two-day 16 hour CSM course or a live-online 14 hour CSM course with one of our certified trainers and/or coaches. Upon completing the training, you will receive a certification account on our website where you will be able to obtain the online test.
- Although we recognize that individuals may have prior experience with the Scrum framework or received training from a different Scrum-certifying body, the CSM test is not intended to be a substitute for formal training from Scrum Alliance®. Those who earn a Certified Scrum Master designation demonstrate a clear opinion

of the CSM Learning objectives addressed in the in-person course.

- Please note that all approved courses that lead to CSM certification are found on our Course Search page; they must be taught by a Certified Scrum Trainer®, Certified Team Coach®, and/or Certified Enterprise Coach®. If you found a CSM class through a third-party, please ensure it is listed on our Course Search page or contact support@scrumalliance.org to ensure its validity toward Scrum Alliance's CSM certification.

Can I retake the CSM® test if I score poorly?

- The CSM test has 50 multiple-choice questions with a passing score of 74%. You will have two free attempts within 90 days and within these days you will receive your initial welcome email to pass the test at no cost. After two attempts and/or 90 days, you will be prompted to pay $25 USD for each additional attempt.
- Please note that if you've already passed the CSM test, you will not be able to take it again to receive a better score. Your test score is only accessible to you; your instructor or other certificates are not able to see how you performed on the CSM test.

CSM Syllabus Outline:

- Prepare at least three rights and five responsibilities of the Product Owner, Development Team, and Scrum Master.
- Explain at least two reasons why the Product Owner is a single person and not a group or a committee.
- Explain how and why the Product Owner maintains authority over the product while working collaboratively with the Development Team and stakeholders.
- Prepare at least five characteristics of the Development Team.

Scrum Events and Artifact Transparency

- Provide one example of how a Scrum Team will inspect and adapt and increase transparency at each of the Scrum events.
- Describe at least three responsibilities for the Development Team, Product Owner, and Scrum Master during Sprint Planning, Daily Scrum, Sprint Review, and Retrospective.

Sprint and Increment

- Clarify why the Sprint Goal does not change during a Sprint.
- Describe the outcome of every Sprint.

- Explain at least three reasons why the increment must be brought to the current definition of 'Done' regardless of whether the Product Owner chooses to release the increment.

Sprint Planning

- 10. Discuss the focus of the activities of the Product Owner and Development Team during the two topics of Sprint Planning: the 'What' and the 'How.'
- 11. Practice writing a Sprint Goal.

Daily Scrum

- Explain at least three ways the Daily Scrum differs from a status meeting and why the various constraints exist to support the Development Team.

Sprint Review

- Describe at least three activities that occur during the Sprint Review other than; a demonstration of the increment.
- Classify at least three potential outcomes for a Sprint Review.

Sprint Retrospective

- Describe at least two approaches to conduct a Sprint Retrospective.

Product Backlog

- Identify at least three essential characteristics of the Product Backlog.
- List at least four attributes of a Product Backlog item.

Sprint Backlog

- Identify at least three essential characteristics of the Sprint Backlog.
- Describe how the Sprint Backlog can be changed without endangering the Sprint Goal.

Definition of "Done"

- Describe the importance of a strong definition of "Done" and describe at least two risks associated with a weaker definition of "Done."
- Outline at least one way to create a definition of "Done." Knowledge Comprehension Application Analysis Synthesis
- Identify at least two reasons why multiple teams working on the same Product Backlog have a shared and consistent definition of "Done."

Scrum Master Core Competencies

Facilitation

- Describe at least three situations in which the Scrum Master could serve the needs of the Scrum Team or organization through facilitation.
- Demonstrate at least three techniques for facilitating group decision making.

Coaching

- Restate how facilitating, teaching, mentoring, and coaching is different.
- Apply at least one technique that could help resolve a challenge faced by a Scrum Team.

Service to the Development Team

Scrum Master as Servant-Leader

- Define servant-leadership.
- Describe three scenarios where the Scrum Master acts as the servant-leader for the Development Team.
- Identify possible violations of Scrum by a Product Owner or stakeholder who is applying excessive time pressure and illustrate how to address them.
- Define technical debt and explain the impact of accumulating technical debt.

- List at least three development practices that will help Scrum Teams deliver a high-quality Product Increment and reduce technical debt each Sprint.

Service to the Product Owner

- Explain at least three ways the Scrum Master could support the Product Owner.
- List at least two benefits that arise if a Product Owner participates in the Sprint Retrospective.

Service to the Organization

Impediment Removal

- Discuss at least two ways that the Scrum Master assists the Scrum Team with impediments.
- Describe at least three organizational impediments that can affect Scrum Teams.

Coaching the Organization

- Describe at least one example of an organizational design change caused by adopting Scrum.
- Discuss why Scrum does not have a project manager and what happens to traditional project management activities.

Knowledge Comprehension Application Analysis Synthesis

CSM Domains	**CSM should demonstrate knowledge of**	**% of CSM test**
A.SCRUM AND AGILE	Four values of Agile Manifesto	
	Twelve Principles of Agile Manifesto	6%
	Definition of Scrum	
	Relationship of Scrum to Agile	
B.SCRUM Theory	Empirical process control as it relates to scrum	
	The 3 pillars of empirical process control and its importance	
	How and why "incremental" is an important characteristic of Scrum	6%

	How and why "iterative" is an important characteristic of Scrum	
	Applicability of Scrum (addresses complex adaptive problems across multiple industries)	
C.SCRUM Values	Identify the five Scrum values	
	How and why commitment is an important Scrum value	6%
	How and why courage is an important Scrum value	
	How and why focus is an important Scrum value	
	How and why openness is an important Scrum value	
	How and why respect is an important Scrum value	
D.SCRUM Team	Why self-organizing is an important characteristic of Scrum teams	
	Why cross-functional is an important characteristic of Scrum teams	

	Identify the roles on the Scrum team	
	Identify the responsibilities and characteristics of the Scrum Master	20%
	Identify the responsibilities and characteristics of the Scrum Product Owner	
	Identify the responsibilities and characteristics of the Scrum Development Team	
E.SCRUM MASTER	Understanding responsibilities and characteristics of the Scrum Master -- servant leader for the Scrum team	
	Scrum Master service to the Organization -- coaching, facilitation, removing impediments	22%
	Scrum Master service to the Development Team -- coaching, facilitation, removing impediments	
	Scrum Master service to the Product Owner -- coaching, facilitation, removing impediments	

F.SCRUM EVENTS	Characteristics, value and/or purpose of the Sprint	
	Sprint Planning -- characteristics, value, purpose and/or role of participants	
	Daily Scrum -- characteristics, value, purpose and/or role of participants	20%
	Sprint Review -- characteristics, value, purpose and/or role of participants	
	Retrospective -- characteristics, value, purpose and/or role of participants	
G.SCRUM ARTIFACTS	Understand the purpose and value of Scrum artifacts	
	Identify Scrum artifacts	
	Product Backlog - characteristics, value and purpose	
	Sprint Backlog -- characteristics, value and purpose	20%

	Increment -- characteristics, value and purpose	
	Understanding importance of transparency of artifacts to evaluate value and risk	
	Identify the downsides of lack of transparency	
	Importance of establishing the definition of "Done"	
	Characteristics of Product Backlog items	

Certified Scrum Master - CSM® EXAM

Resource and Study Guide for the CSM® (Certified Scrum Master) Exam

Thiyagarajan Perumal MBA, PMP, PMI-ACP, CSM, ITIL, 6 Sigma Black Belt, PRINCE2 Practitioner, CBAP

- **If you're preparing to take the CSM® Exam, on your way to earning a CSM® (Certified Scrum Master) certification, you must download this useful resource.**
- **You are guaranteed to find these and more from the CSM® - EXAM PREP, your ticket to passing your CSM® exam.**

The author, a CSM himself, has compiled the necessary information into a single, concise course to

help you achieve your goals. He has been in your shoes, felt the stresses that are inherent in trying to advance a career, and knows the value of time. His thought process, in creating this unique guide, is to offer his expertise and resources as a helping hand to those moving into the field.

Master the Knowledge and Information Needed to Pass – Without Fail

- **For those who know the information, but under the pressure of taking the exam, choke and stumble to get the answers out, there is a section on exam strategies. Consider some methods that will make writing the exam easier. Build your confidence going into the exam by knowing what to expect and how to cope, should you falter.**

About the book:

- **Whether you are a beginner or near the point of taking the certification exam, you will find this book beneficial. It can be used to prep you along the way, assuring your success when you do challenge the exam. Take a look at what is included:**

5 Fully Simulated Practice Exam with Detailed Answer & Explanation

Total 300 + Questions with Answers

- **It's an essential resource for Information Technology (IT) Project Managers, and anyone practicing the Project Management & Agile Principles/Manifesto, SCRUM, and CSM® Exam.**

- **It is applicable today and will enhance your chances of passing the first time, with nearly guaranteed success.**
- **A word about the author: Thiyagarajan, as friends and co-workers know him, is passionate about his work and life, in general. He's traveled these same educational roads and knows the importance of setting and achieving goals. As a highly certified leader in the Agile/SCRUM community, he is offering his help to further the education of new students, adding vitality and 'new blood' to the profession.**
- **Don't hesitate to build self-confidence, save valuable time, and take the next step to fulfil your career goals – purchase Thiyagarajan' s book and set the worry aside.**

TIME TO LEARN

Key Concepts In Scrum/Agile:

Scrum Team: Product Owner, Development Team, and **Scrum** Master, together these are known as the **Scrum** Team.

3 Roles in Scrum: Product owner, Development Team, Scrum master

5 Scrum Value are,

- Commitment
- Openness
- Courage
- Respect
- Focus

3 Pillars of Scrum: 3 pillars of scrum are, transparency, inspection and adoption.

Agile Manifesto: Individuals and Interactions over process and tools

Working software over comprehensive documentation

Customer collaboration over contract negotiation

Responding to Change over following a plan.

The value on the left is more important than on the right.

Agile Principles:

1. Our highest priority is to satisfy the customer through early and continuous delivery of valuable software

2. Welcome changing requirements, even late in development. Agile process harness change for the customer's competitive advantage.

3. Deliver working software frequently from a couple of weeks to a couple of months with a preference to the shorter time scale.

4. Business people and developers must work together daily throughout the project

5. Build projects around motivated individuals. Give them the environment and support they need, and trust them to get the job done.

6. The most efficient and effective method of conveying information to and within a development team is face-to-face conversation.7. Working software is the primary measure of progress.

8. Agile processes promote sustainable development. The sponsors, developers, and users should be able to maintain a constant pace indefinitely.

9. Continuous attention to technical excellence and good design enhances agility.

10. Simplicity, the art of maximizing the amount of work not done is essential.

11. The best architectures, requirements and designs emerge from self-organizing teams.

12. At regular intervals, the team reflects on how to become more effective, then tunes and adjusts its behavior accordingly.

Difference between Scrum, Kanban and agile processes are,

Kanban: Kanban process is mainly for process improvements

Scrum: Scrum concerned about more work done faster

Agile: iterative methods breaks projects into smaller parts

5 Scrum Ceremonies (event) are,

- Sprint backlog/Product backlog
- Sprint planning meeting
- Daily scrum meeting
- Sprint review meeting
- Sprint retrospective meeting

3 empirical process control in Scrum

- Transparency
- Inspection
- Adaptation

Sprint Planning:

- During the sprint planning meeting, the product owner describes the highest priority features to the team.
- The Scrum team asks enough questions that they can turn a high-level user story of the product backlog into the more detailed tasks of the sprint backlog.
- The purpose of sprint planning is to define what can be delivered in the sprint and how that work will be achieved.

Roles & Responsibilities of Product owner

- Defining the vision
- Represent the customer
- Acting as primary liaison between customer and stakeholders
- Managing the product backlog
- Prioritizing needs of customer
- Overseeing development stages
- Anticipating client needs
- Evaluating product progress at each iteration

Purpose of sprint: to accomplish a task

Scrum Master Roles and Responsibilities:

- Scrum master ensures that the team follows the scrum process
- He/She deals with impediments in the project
- He/She work with product owner to create the backlog for the next sprint

PRACTICE EXAMS:

It is time for a Practice Examination!!!

CSM (Certified Scrum Master) Practice Exam 1:

1. Which Scrum meeting given below is time-boxed for 4 hours?

1. Sprint planning meeting
2. Release planning meeting
3. Retrospective meeting
4. Daily standup meeting

2. Which one of the below questions not asked in the daily stand up meeting?

A. What have you done since the last meeting?
B. Check the product status from all the members of an agile team
C. What are you planning to do now and between the next meetings?
D. Is there any obstacle in the way?

3. The meeting which is held at the end of each iteration?

A. Review meeting (Product based)
B. Retrospective meeting (process-based)
C. A and B
D. Team happy hour

4. One of the given options not a valid job role of Scrum Master?

A. Ensure the process is followed

B. shields the team from interruptions
C. Assign job to the team
D. Remove impediments that block progress

5. Not a valid agile manifesto?

A. Processes and tools over individual and interactions
B. working software over comprehensive documentation
C. customer collaboration over contract negotiation
D. Responding to change over following a plan

6. Who manages the iteration backlog?

A. The product manager
B. The sponsor
C. The team
D. The product owner

7. Not a primary role in Scrum?

A. The product owner
B. The team
C. Project manager
D. Scrum master

8. Who is the single voice of the customer in SCRUM?

A. The project manager
B. The product owner
C. The sponsor

D. The scrum master

9. In SCRUM the responsibility for prioritizing user stories belong to,

A. Belongs to the combined effort of product owner and the team
B. Belongs to the team only
C. Belongs to the product owner
D. it is the responsibility of Scrum Master

10. Agile team members make decisions collaboratively and take ownership of a decision. The decision model is known as?

A. Participatory
B. command and control
C. share decision model
D. individual

11. Through the retrospective, few issues were found. The person is responsible for resolving all the issues?

A. scrum master
B. product owner
C. the entire team
D. project manager

12. The meeting which is held at the end of the iteration, which is product-based

A. Daily standup meeting

B. Team meeting
C. Review meeting
D. Retrospective meeting

13. Definition of done can be created by

A. Team
B. Product owner
C. Scrum master
D. All of the above

14. According to agile manifesto, which one of the below is a valid combination related to individuals and interactions

A. over following a plan
B. over contract negotiation
C. over comprehensive documentation
D. over process and tools

15. According to the agile principle, one of the below is the primary measure of progress

A. extensive documentation
B. working software
C. good architecture
D. encouraging work environment

16. Ideal team member location in agile Projects?

A. colocation
B. virtual

C. Distributed
D. Global

17. Your scrum team completed 20 story points in the recent 4 releases. What is your team's velocity?

1. A.80
2. B.20
3. C.5
4. D.24

18. Characteristics of a high-performance team

A. Self-organized team
B. Trust each other
C. Both A and B
D. None of the above

19. Servant leadership roles are

A. Shield team from interruptions
B. remove obstacles
C. communicate the project vision
D. All of the above

20. One of the benefits of retrospectives of the agile team is

A. improved productivity
B. improved quality
C. improved capacity
D. all of the above

21. When it is necessary to split the user story?

A. Whenever the Scrum master want to split the user story
B. Not necessary to split the user story
C. The user story is large to fit within a single iteration
D. None of them

22. Under the Scrum framework, all the activities are time-boxed. Time boxed plan in the Scrum framework is called

A. Product scope is committed, but the release date is not confirmed
B. Both the product scope and release date are confirmed in advance.
C. The release date is committed, but the features to be developed for the release is not defined.
D. None of the above

23. If the defects found are very late in the agile project, it causes

A. less expensive
B. more expensive
C. It is not making any difference in cost
D. None of the above

24. The agile manifesto which is considered team empowerment

A. Individuals and interactions over process and tools
B. Working software over comprehensive documentation
C. customer collaboration over contract negotiation
D. Responding to change over following a plan

25. When is a product roadmap created in an agile project?

A. At the beginning of the release
B. At the beginning of the iteration
C. During sprint review
D. At the beginning of the project

26. Advantages of a collocated team in agile

A. closer working relationship
B. collaboration
C. enables face-to-face communication
D. All of the above

27. Meaning of done in agile project

A. Coded
B. Tested
C. Defect-free
D. All of the above

28. The team meeting used to synchronize their team activities and report any impediments that block the progress is called

A. product demo
B. daily standup meeting
C. retrospective meeting
D. status meeting

29. Team meetings held at the end of every iteration in Scrum is called

A. Status meeting, review meeting
B. review meeting, retrospective meeting
C. team meeting, review meeting
D. The retrospective meeting, Daily standup meeting

30. _______________ is used to quantify the work effort and complexity required to develop a user story related to other stories

A. story card
B. user stories
C. story points
D. none of the above

31. PMO management asked the agile team for a detailed project plan. The response of the Scrum master should be,

A. Tell the management that plan is not needed for the agile project
B. Request the team to stop the work, and prepare the detailed project plan

C. prepare the detailed project plan
D. Take the opportunity to educate the senior management on agile principles

32. Identify the chart that shows the work remaining in story points or ideal days in the project.

A. burn up chart
B. dashboard
C. burn down chart
D. product vision box

33. User stories at the top of the backlog in

A. not well defined
B. well defined
C. prioritized
D. Not-prioritized

34. Product backlog in scrum should be

A. Detailed
B. Estimated
C. Prioritized
D. All of the above

35. Lessons learned in the scrum project happens during

A. During only the first few iterations
B. During the product demo
C. Throughout the project duration

D. Only after the project failure during the post review session

36. Which agile methodology is widely used?

A. Scrum
B. lean
C. XP
D. Kanban

37. Which one of these statements reflects the agile principle?

A. Projects built around process rather than products
B. Projects are built around technical coding expert
C. Projects are built around motivated individuals
D. Projects are built around the project manager's choice

38. Is the person responsible to write user stories?

A. The product owner
B. The tester
C. The customer
D. Project manager

39. How often the entire agile/scrum team meet on the project?

A. Once weekly
B. Daily

C. At the beginning of each iteration
D. Depends on the agreement on team member and product owner

40. Estimating the effort of user stories will be represented by?

A. cycle time
B. ideal days
C. velocity
D. calendar days

41. The best definition of done is defined as?

A. Determined by the project manager
B. Determined by customer
C. Determined by the team
D. Determined by the scrum master

42. Which values are a secondary value in the agile manifesto?

A. Contract negotiation
B. working software
C. customer collaboration
D. responding to change

43. What is the story point in scrum?

A. A fixed unit of development effort
B. A unit of work

C. How the user story is described and assign a number to that?
D. A fixed unit of the testing effort

44. Which one of the following is an agile feedback technique?

A. Finding a defect
B. Prototyping
C. source code review
D. Team meeting

45. What is meant by an empowered team?

A. A team takes ownership of a product and is collectively responsible for its delivery.
B. The project manager makes decisions for the team
C. Product owner told how to develop user stories?
D. The team always got instructions from higher authority regarding the decisions.

46. The total number of story points to be completed is 45. The number of team members in the agile team is 6. The velocity of the team is 5. How many iterations will it take for the team to complete 45 story points?

A. 5
B. 7
C. 8

D. 9

47. The document that holds a list of features to be developed in the project?

A. Sprint backlog
B. product backlog
C. iteration backlog
D. release list

48. Which scrum meeting is time-boxed to 4 hours?

A. Release plan meeting
B. sprint review meeting
C. retrospective meeting
D. daily scrum meeting

49. Remove obstacles for the team is the responsibility of scrum master. By removing obstacles, we are eliminating

A. roadblocks
B. impediments
C. project risk
D. none of the above

50. What is the duration of iteration?

A. One month
B. One week
C. 2 to 4 weeks
D. Depends on the project

CSM PRACTICE EXAM 1: ANSWERS

1. Answer: A

- Sprint planning meeting time-boxed for 4 hours
- Release planning meeting typically between 4 to 8 hours
- The retrospective meeting lasts up to 1 hour
- Daily standup meeting generally lasts for 15 minutes

2. Answer: B

- In Daily stand-up meeting 3 questions should be asked in general. 1. What did you work yesterday? 2. What are you going to work on today? 3. is there any impediments are you encountering?

3. Answer: C

- 2 meetings generally held at the end of the iteration. Review meeting (product based) and Retrospective meeting (process-based)

4. Answer: C

- Except for option C, other roles are valid job roles for a scrum master. Assign job to the team members are not the responsibility of Scrum master. The team self organizes and assigns the tasks between themselves.

5. Answer: A

- The valid agile manifesto is individuals and interactions over the process and tools. Working software over comprehensive documentation. Customer collaboration over contract negotiation. Responding to a changeover following a plan.
- Option A is not correct. It should be individuals and interactions over processes and tools.

6. Answer: C

- Items selected from the product backlog for the particular iteration. Prioritized user stories in the product backlog that the team is committed to developing during a particular iteration.

7. Answer: C

- The product owner usually writes the user stories, and responsible for the product backlog. They are also responsible for backlog grooming and prioritization of user stories between iterations.
- The team is responsible for the product, which is self-organizing and tasks are not assigned to them. Scrum Master to help the team to follow the process, and remove impediments on the

way. Option C is not a valid primary role in the Scrum.

8. Answer B.

- The product owner is the single point of contact for customers in Scrum. They are the voice of customers and representatives, stakeholders, and business, setting priorities and deliverables. Other choices PM, sponsor, and scrum master are not correct.

9. Answer: A

- The responsibility for prioritizing the user stories belongs to the joint effort of the product owner and the team. Other options are not correct.

10. Answer: A

- The decision model where agile team members make decisions collaboratively and take ownership of the decision. This decision model is known as participatory decision making. Other options are not correct.

11. Answer: C

- Issues found during the retrospective are process-based. This needs to be resolved by the entire agile team.

12. Answer: C

- A product-based meeting, which is held at the end of each iteration is called a review meeting. The retrospective meeting is held at the end of all iterations and it is process-based. The agile team identifies the ways to improve its performance through a retrospective. Agile/Scrum team has a daily standup meeting, which occurs at the same time, same place for 15 minutes to synchronize team members' activities. It won't happen at the end of the iteration. Options A, B, and D are not valid choices.
- The activity that a team reviews its performance to improve its performance. Held at the end of every iteration, and it is a process-centric meeting. During the retrospective, the team reflects on what happened in the iteration and identifies actions for improvement going forward.
- A daily standup meeting is to synchronize the team member's activities.

13. Answer: D

- The definition of done can be jointly created by the team, product owner, and the scrum master.

14. Answer: D

- Individuals and interactions over process and tools. Other options A, B, C are not correct.

15. Answer: B

- According to agile principle working software is the primary measure of progress.
- Documentation also needed, only barely sufficient enough. Good architecture and encouraging working environment are not valid choices.
- Ideally, the entire team would be sitting in the same room so that there are no barriers (no matter how small) to communicate. When team members are spread out over different rooms, locations, or time zones, it is normal for people to postpone their interaction

16. Answer: A

- The team benefits from Osmotic communication by collocating its team members. Collocation is the ideal agile team location. Virtual, global, and distributed are not ideal team member locations in agile.
- As it turns out, Agile experts are not all aligned on the optimal agile team size. Most Agile and Scrum training courses refer to a 7 +/- 2 rule, that is, agile or Scrum teams should be 5 to 9

members. Scrum enthusiasts may recall that the Scrum guide says Scrum teams should not be less than 3 or more than 9.

17. Answer: D

- The average number of story points completed per iteration is called velocity. In this case, the Scrum team completed 20 story points in the last 4 releases. So the team velocity is 20.

18. Answer: C

- Some of the characteristics of a high-performance team are self-organized, committed team, trust each other member of the team. The team has empowered to make the decisions and not wait for the manager to take decisions. The team participates in all major decision making. Team decisions are based on the consensus-driven.

19. Answer: D

- The primary duties of the leader serving the team are to shield the team from interruptions, remove obstacles to progress, communicate project vision to the team, and carry food and water (providing essential resources to keep the team productive).

20. Answer: D

- The benefits of retrospectives of the agile team are improved productivity, improved quality, improved capacity, and improved capability.

21. Answer: C

Sometimes the user story is too large to fit in a single iteration. At those times we need to split the user story

22. Answer: C

In a time-boxed plan, the release date is committed, but the features to be developed for the iteration is not defined.

Under the Scrum framework, all activities are time-boxed, also known as "time boxing" or time boxed, is to give a "fixed length" time segment to a specific event or activity. That unit of time is called a time box. The goal of time boxing is to define and limit the amount of time dedicated to an activity.

23. Answer: B

- If we find the defects very late in the project, it is more expensive to fix it. If we find defects very early in the project phase, it is less expensive to fix.
- Progress on a Scrum project can be tracked by means of a release burn down chart. A burn

down chart is a graphical representation of work left to do versus time. It is often used in agile software development methodologies such as Scrum. Its purpose is to enable that the project is on the track to deliver the expected solution within the desired schedule. Burn down charts reinforce the Scrum values of commitment, focus and openness, and transparency. It is updated at the daily scrum.

24. Answer: A

- Individuals and interactions over process and tools, this manifesto related to team empowerment.

25. Answer: D

- It is created at the beginning of the project. It is not created during the sprint review. Also, a product roadmap is not created at the beginning of the release or iteration.

26. Answer: D

- Having a co-located team improve communication, closer working relationship, and collaboration and enables face-to-face communication.

27. Answer: D

- Done-done means the product is coded, tested, defect-free, and accepted by the product owner.
- A term often used by teams to mean the work performed during the sprint is "really" done. Done to the point where the customer would think the work is done

28. Answer: B

- Product demo occurs on the last day of the iteration. The purpose of the meeting is for the team to show the customers and stakeholders the work they have done in the current iteration. The meeting is facilitated by the product owner.

29. Answer: B

- 2 meetings team held at the end of each iteration, Review meeting, and retrospective meeting.
- During the review meeting potentially shippable product increment is presented to stakeholders for their review. This review meeting is a product based meeting. The retrospective meeting is process-based. In this meeting, the team identifies the ways to improve deliverables. Option B is the correct answer. Other options are not correct.

30. Answer: C

- Story points used to quantify the work effort and complexity required to develop a user story related to other stories. Other options are not correct.

31. Answer: D

- Management asked the project team a detailed project plan. Agile coach uses this as an opportunity to educate senior management on agile principles. Other options are not correct.

32. Answer: C

- Burn down chart

33. Answer: B

- User stories at the top of the backlog are well defined. Other options are not correct.

34. Answer: D

- The product backlog should be detailed, estimable, emerging, and prioritized.

35. Answer: C

- Option C is the correct answer. Lessons learned should be captured throughout the project by the team. If something good or bad happens during the project, the team remembers when it is fresh and forget key details after some time.

36. Answer: A

- Scrum is the widest methodology available in the market.

37. Answer: C

- Other options are wrong. In agile projects are built around motivated individuals in the team.

38. Answer: A

- The product owner is responsible to write user stories. They serve as a connection between the customer and the team. They are responsible to write user stories and prioritize them. Tester/customer/PM is not responsible to write user stories.

39. Answer: B

- The entire agile team meets daily. The team has a daily standup meeting, which occurs daily at the same time, same place for 15 minutes to synchronize team member's activities. All other choices are not correct for the agile teams.

40. Answer: B

- Story size specified by ideal days, actual days, story points. It is the time required to complete the activity, assuming there are no interruptions so that work can be completed 100% efficient.

- Cycle time is not used for estimating user stories. It is the time taken to complete the work from start to finish.
- Velocity is used to find the number of user stories that a team can deliver within an iteration. Calendar days are not used to estimate the effort of user stories.

41. Answer C.

- It is determined by the team.

42. Answer: A

- Agile manifesto (Highlighted values on the right-hand side are secondary values)
- Individuals and interactions over process and tools
- Working software over comprehensive documentation
- Customer collaboration over contract negotiation
- Responding to change over following a plan

43. Answer: A

- It is a fixed unit of development effort. Used to quantify the work effort and complexity required to develop a user story related to other stories.

- Options B, C, and D are not correct answers.
- A story point is a metric used in agile project management and development to estimate the difficulty of implementing a given user story, which is an abstract measure of effort required to implement it. In simple terms, a story point is a number that tells the team about the difficulty level of the story.

44. Answer: B

- Prototyping is one of the agile feedback techniques for the product. The prototype is used to get valuable feedback from the user early in the project. Finding defects, source code review, and team meetings are not feedback techniques in agile.

45. Answer: A

- An empowered team takes ownership of a product and is collectively responsible for its delivery. Decision authority belongs to the entire team and not related to any single individual.
- Option B, Option C is wrong. If PM or product owner makes decisions for the team it is not empowered. A team that always got instruction from higher authority regarding the decision is also not an empowered team.

46. Answer: D

- The total number of story points/velocity (45/5) = 9. The team will complete the story points in 9 iterations.

47. Answer: B

- Both sprint backlog and iteration backlog holds a list of product features, to be developed in the sprint/iteration. The release list is not a valid choice. Only product backlog holds a list of product features to be developed in the project.

48. Answer: B

- Sprint review meeting time-boxed for 4 hours
- Release plan meeting typically lasts between 4 and 8 hours
- The retrospective meeting generally lasts up to 1 hour.
- Daily standup meeting generally lasts up to 15 minutes.

49. Answer: C

- By the way of removing obstacles/impediments, we are eliminating the risk of the agile project.

50. Answer: C

- In general, iteration is between 2 to 4 weeks.

CSM (Certified Scrum Master) PRACTICE EXAM 2:

1. Which is not a valid agile empirical process?

a. Transparency
b. inspection
c. adoption
d. validation

2. When a team is in trust, self-organized, and make decisions collectively, it is called?

A. independent team
B. cross-functional team
C. motivated team
D. empowered team

3. In Scrum methodology which one of the below, serves as a connection between the product owner and the team?

A. The iteration backlog
B. The product backlog
C. Sprint review
D. Elevator statement

4. An agile method to improve motivation?

A. providing guidance
B. providing feedback
C. empowerment
D. conduct team get-together

5. The duty of servant leader?

A. help the product owner
B. leader also a team member
C. work with the team in key project
D. providing support and remove obstacles

6. One of the following is the secondary value in the agile manifesto?

A. individuals and interactions
B. working software
C. customer collaboration
D. following a plan

7. The chart shows the work completed, in story points or ideal days in the project.

A. Burndown chart
B. Burn up chart
C. cumulative flow diagram
D. Dashboard

8. in the agile manifesto

A. The value on the left is more important than the value on the right
B. Value on the right is more important than the value on the left
C. Both the values on the left and right are equal
D. All of the above

9. Which one of the given options is not one of the pillars of SCRUM?

A. adaption
B. inspection
C. sprint review
D. visibility

10. Which one of the below is not of the roles of the SCRUM team?

A. it is a cross-functional team
B. delivers a product in the final SPRINT
C. self-organizing teams
D. members volunteer to the project work

11. The person responsible to define the business value of the feature that the customer wants,

A. Business Analyst
B. Scrum master
C. The product owner/customer proxy
D. SPRINT team

12. One of the ceremonies in SCRUM is a daily scrum meeting. From the given list below, find out the person attending the Daily Scrum meeting?

A. product owner
B. scrum master
C. scrum development team
D. All of the above

13. Team preferred approach for agile development process?

A. Design everything in the beginning
B. Design only enough in the beginning
C. In agile no planning is necessary
D. None of the above

14. Each SPRINT has

A. sprint planning
B. development work
C. sprint review meeting
D. All of the above

15. Product owner responsibility

A. product vision
B. responsible for prioritizing and reprioritizing product backlog
C. Define the user stories
D. All of the above

16. Who should resolve conflicts in the SCRUM development team?

A. Scrum master
B. Scrum development team
C. Product owner
D. Project manager

17. The team size of SCRUM team is,

A. 20
B. 7+ or - 2
C. 3
D. 10

18. Basis Unit of development in Scrum is called as,

A. Scrum of Scrum
B. SPRINT
C. Iteration
D. None of the above

19. One of the below is not a Daily Scrum Guidance,

A. The meeting must be in the same location
B. Scrum master assigns tasks to the Scrum team in this meeting
C. The meeting is always 15 minutes
D. Daily scrum meeting generally at the same time

20. A product backlog is prioritized based on the,

A. business value
B. Risk
C. complexity
D. all of the above

21. One of the below options is not related to the product backlog

A. It is prioritized by the product owner

B. It is colocation of requirements, features, and defects
C. More details are available at the bottom of the backlog
D. More details are available at the top of the backlog

22. Structure of a user story

A. As a <scrum master> I want <feature> so that <value>
B. As a <user> I want <feature> so that <value>
C. As a <project manager> I want <feature> so that <value>
D. None of the above

23. Things to be done, before declaring it is done,

A. Tested
B. Designed
C. Coded
D. All of the above

24. Your Scrum team completed 10 story points, in the recent 4 releases. What is your team's velocity?

A. 2
B. 10
C. 40
D. None of the above

25. According to an agile principle which communication is the most efficient way of communication?

A. email communication
B. informal communication
C. Face-to-face communication
D. Written communication

26. The agile principle suggests the best architecture emerge from

A. System architect
B. enterprise architect
C. Scrum master
D. Self-organizing teams

27. The activity that a team reviews its performance for the purpose of improving its performance for the next iteration?

A. velocity
B. refactor
C. retrospective
D. planning poker

28. The best definition of prioritization?

A. the relative ordering of user stories with respect to value
B. always prioritize, based on the priority of project manager

C. always prioritize based on the priority of product owner
D. the team define the prioritization

29. What is the sprint backlog?

A. A list of features developed in a sprint
B. A list of features developed in multiple sprints
C. features developed in a project
D. features developed in a release

30. The delivery which is used in SCRUM?

A. incremental delivery
B. real-time delivery
C. iteration delivery
D. functionality delivery

31. The document that holds a list of product features to be developed in a project?

A. sprint backlog
B. product backlog
C. iteration backlog
D. release list

32. The type of risk that is managed in agile?

A. qualitative
B. reactive
C. quantitative
D. qualitative and quantitative

33. In the last iteration, your team completed 3 user stories worth of 5 points each, 2 user stories worth of 10 points each, and nearly completed 1 user story which has worth 15 story points. What is your team velocity?

A. 35
B. 50
C. 60
D. 40

34. When a team in trust, and self-organized and makes decisions collectively it is called?

A. independent team
B. cross-functional team
C. motivated team
D. empowered team

35. What is the Scrum Master responsible for?

A. Teaching Scrum and seeing that it is adopted and used correctly.
B. Imposing metrics and managing the performance of the Development Team.
C. The Development Team's meetings and for the objectives the Development Team outlines for itself.
D. Defining the Development Team's tasks during the Sprint.

36. Story size cannot be specified as one of the following

A. ideal days
B. Actual days
C. Story points
D. Iteration Days

37. Not a valid agile empirical process.

A. Transparency
B. Inspection
C. Adaption
D. Validation

38. One of the following is not a valid job role of agile manager

A. Ensure the process is followed
B. Shields the team from interruption
C. Assign jobs to the team
D. Remove impediments that block progress

39. What is not a primary role in the Scrum?

A. product owner
B. the team
C. project manager
D. scrum master

40. In Agile responsibility for prioritizing user stories belong to

A. belongs to the combined effort of the product owner and the team
B. Belongs to the team only
C. Belongs to the product owner
D. It is the responsibility of scrum master

41. During the Retrospective session, few issues were found. The person is responsible for resolving all the issues?

A. scrum owner
B. product owner
C. the entire team
D. project manager

42. The meetings held at the end of the iteration, which is product-based

A. daily standup meeting
B. team meeting
C. review meeting
D. retrospective meeting

43. one of the following is not a feedback cycle in agile?

A. project planning meeting
B. iteration review meeting
C. retrospective meeting

D. daily standup meeting

44. The team meeting used to synchronize their team activities and report any impediments that block the progress is called

A. product demo
B. daily standup meeting
C. retrospective meeting
D. status meeting

45. The best architectures, requirements, and designs emerge from one of the following,

A. product owner
B. scrum master
C. self-organizing teams
D. from subject matter experts

46. The agile principle related to changes,

A. Agile isn't welcoming changes in requirement after the project is started.
B. Agile welcome changing requirements, even late in development.
C. In agile changes to requirements would go through a strict change control process and get approval from many departments.
D. In agile before the project start, the requirements are finalized and base lined. All changes go through the change control process.

47. According to the agile principle, one of the below is the primary measure of progress,

A. extensive documentation
B. working software
C. good architecture
D. encouraging work environment

48. Not one of the Responsibilities of product owner,

A. They are responsible to write user stories.

B. Remove the obstacles/impediments for the team.

C. Voice of the customer and representing stakeholders and business.

D. Prioritize the user stories.

49. The nature of work done on iteration 0

A. No new work is done during this iteration.
B. Only the next few iterations are planned in detail, more distant are planned at a higher level.
C. Team present work product to stakeholders, so that they can review the product and give feedback.
D. To do all those things that your project is ready to start like, develop product backlog, having a release plan.

50. The person who owns the product changes are

A. The team

B. Scrum master
C. The product owner
D. D.XP team

CSM PRACTICE EXAM 2: ANSWERS

1. Answer: D

- Valid empirical processes are Transparency, Inspection, and adoption. Option D is not a valid agile empirical process.

2. Answer: D

- An empowered team takes ownership of a product and is collectively responsible for its delivery. Decision authority belongs to the entire team and is not related to any single individual.
- The cross-functional team does not make decisions like an empowered team
- The Independent team and motivated team are not the correct answer.

3. Answer: B

- The product backlog serves as a connection between the product owner and the team.
- The iteration backlog is limited to one iteration.
- The sprint review is after every sprint, to review the product. This option is also not correct.

- Elevator statements are brief and can be shared with the fellow elevator passenger, explain the project vision in the short amount of time it takes to ride an elevator from one floor to another. This option also not correct.

4. Answer: C

- Providing guidance/feedback is not an agile concept.
- A team takes ownership of a product and is collectively responsible for its delivery. Since the team collectively takes the decision, they try to give their best.
- Option D is also not the correct answer.

5. Answer: D

- Options A, B, and C are not the duties of a servant leader. Providing support and removing obstacles are the duties of the servant leader.

6. Answer: D

- Individuals and interactions over process and tools
- Working software over comprehensive documentation
- Customer collaboration over contract negotiation
- Responding to change over following a plan

- The value on the left is more important than that on the right. Right-hand side values are secondary values.

7. Answer: B

- The chart shows the work completed, in story points or ideal days in the project is called burn-up charts. Other options are not correct.

8. Answer: A

- In an agile manifesto, the value on the left is more important than the right. All other options are not correct.

9. Answer: C

- Three pillars of Scrum are visibility, inspection, and adaption. Option C is not the correct answer. The sprint review is one of the Sprint ceremonies.

10. Answer: B

- The scrum team is cross-functional, and it is self-organized and selects the work according to their skills. Option C is the correct answer. Other options are not correct.

11. Answer: C

- The product owner is the single point of contact for customers in the scrum. They are the voice of the customers and represents the stakeholders and business, setting priorities, and deliverables. They are the ones who define the features that the customer wants. Other options A, B, and D are not correct.

12. Answer: D

- Option D is the correct answer. The entire Scrum team meets daily. The team has a daily scrum meeting, which occurs daily at the same time, same place for 15 minutes to synchronize team member's activities and plan accordingly.

13. Answer: B

- For the preferred approach for agile planning, minimum upfront design, which is necessary for the iteration is enough. No need to plan everything in detail like a plan-driven approach. Option B is the correct choice. Other options are not correct.

14. Answer: D

- Each Sprint has sprint planning, development work, Daily scrum meeting, SPRINT review meeting, Sprint Retrospective. Option D is the correct answer.

15. Answer: D

- The product owner is responsible for product vision and responsible for prioritizing and reprioritizing product backlog. They answer questions related to the product requirements to the development team. They can decide whether to accept or reject the project.

16. Answer: B

- The scrum team is self-organized and empowered to make decisions. Scrum master won't involve in the process of resolving the conflict. But they can assist with the team in resolving the conflict. The scrum team itself will resolve the conflicts. Other options A, C, and D are not correct.

17. Answer: B

- Generally, the scrum team size is 7 + or – 2. Option B is the correct option.

18. Answer: B

- The basic unit of development in Scrum is called as the SPRINT. Sprint lasts between 1 week to 1 month mostly.

- Option C is the basic unit of development in agile.
- Option A Scrum of Scrum, it is a meeting of multiple scrum teams, typically attended by the scrum master or a designated representative.

19. Answer: B

- Option B is not the guidelines for the Scrum team. The task is not assigned to the scrum team, the team is self-organized and assigns the task to themselves. Another option A, C, and D are the daily scrum guidelines.

20. Answer: D

- A product backlog is prioritized based on business value, risk, complexity, and demand. Option D is the correct answer.

21. Answer: C

- Option C is not correct related to the product backlog. Only more details are available at the top of the product backlog, which is going to be completed in the current Sprint.
- Option A is correct, always it is prioritized by the product owner
- Option B is also correct. A backlog is the collection of requirements, features, and defects.

- Option D is also correct. More details about the features/requirements are available at the top of the product backlog.

22. Answer: B

- Option B is the correct choice. The structure of the user story is,
- As a user, I want <feature> so that <value>. Other options are not correct.

23. Answer: D

- Option D is the correct choice. Things that need to be done, before it is declared as done are tested, coded, designed, installed, reviewed, and accepted.

24. Answer: B

- The average number of story points completed per Sprint is called velocity. As per the given scenario, it is 10 story points are the team's velocity. Other options are not correct.

25. Answer: C

- One of the key agile principle, the most efficient and effective method of conveying information to and within a development team is face-to-face conversation. Option C is correct. Other options A, B, D are not correct.

26. Answer: D

- The agile principle suggests, the best architectures, requirements, and designs emerge from self-organizing teams. Option D is the correct option. Other options A, B, and C are not correct.

27. Answer: C

- Retrospective used for the process improvement in the teamwork. During the retrospective, the team reflects on what happened in the iteration and identifies actions for improvement going forward.
- Velocity is the number of user stories that a team delivers within the iteration and is not related to performance.
- Refactor is restructuring the code, without changing the external behavior of the code and not a performance-related review for the team.
- Planning poker is one of the agile techniques used to estimate the story points of a user story and it is not related to the performance-related review for the team.

28. Answer: C

- The product owner defines the prioritization.

29. Answer: A

- Choices B, C, and D are wrong. It means the relative ordering of user stories concerning the value.

30. Answer: A.

- The delivery which is used in agile is incremental. The product is delivered in increments in iterations. Options B, C, and D are not valid choices.

31. Answer: B

- Both sprint backlog and iteration backlog holds a list of product features, to be developed in the sprint/iteration. The release list is not a valid choice. Only product backlog holds a list of product features, to be developed in the project.

32. Answer: A

- Only qualitative risks are managed in agile. All other options are not correct.

33. Answer: A

- (3*5 + 2*10 = 35). Option A is the right answer. The nearly completed user story is not taken into account for velocity calculation.

34. Answer: D

An empowered team takes ownership of a product and is collectively responsible for its delivery. Decision authority belongs to the entire team and is not related to any single individual.

The cross-functional team does not make decisions like an empowered team.

35. Answer A.

- Teaching Scrum and seeing that it is adopted and used correctly.

36. Answer: D.

- Option D is not the correct option. Story size can be specified in ideal days, actual days, and story points.

37. Answer: D

- Explanation: Valid agile empirical process is Transparency, inspection, and adoption. Option D is not a valid agile empirical process.

38. Answer: C.

- Explanation: Except for option C, other choices are valid roles of the agile manager. Assign jobs to the team members are not the responsibility of the agile team manager. The team self organizes and assigns the tasks between themselves.

39. Answer: C

- Explanation: The product owner usually writes the user stories, and responsible for the product backlog. They are also responsible for backlog grooming and prioritization of user stories between iterations. The team is responsible for the product which is self-organizing, and tasks are not assigned to them. Scrum Master helps the team to follow the process, and remove impediments on the way. Option C is not a valid primary role in the scrum.

40. Answer: A

- Explanation: Option A is the correct choice. The responsibility for prioritizing the user stories belongs to the joint effort of the team and product owner. Option B, Option C, and Option D are not correct.

41. Answer: C.

- Explanation: Issues found during retrospectives are process-based. This issue needs to be resolved by the entire agile team. Option C is the correct answer.

42. Answer: C

- Explanation: Product based meeting, which is held at the end of each iteration is called Review meeting. The retrospective meeting is held at the end of alliteration and it is process-based. Agile Team identifies the ways to improve its performance through a retrospective. The agile team has a daily stand up meeting, which occurs daily at the same time, same place for 15 minutes to synchronize team member's activities. It won't happen at the end of the iteration. Options A, B, and D are not valid choices.

43. Answer: A.

- Explanation: Retrospective is one of the feedback cycles, which is used to improve team performance. Daily stand up meeting also one of the agile feedback cycles and is conducted mainly to synchronize team member's activities. It is used to identify the issues before they become problematic. At the Iteration Review meeting, the team presents the work product to stakeholders, so that they can review the product and give feedback. Option A is not a valid feedback cycle in agile.

44. Answer: B

- Explanation: Product Demo occurs on the last day of the iteration. The purpose of the meeting is for the team to show the customers and stakeholders the work they have done in the current iteration. The meeting is facilitated by the product owner. The activity that a team reviews its performance to improve its performance. Held at the end of every iteration. Process centric meeting. During the retrospective, the team reflects on what happened in the iteration and identifies actions for improvement going forward. A daily standup meeting is to synchronize the team member's activities. Option B is the correct choice.

45. Answer: C.

- Explanation: According to the agile principle, the best architectures, requirements, and designs emerge from self-organizing teams. Option C is the correct choice. All other options are not correct.

46. Answer: B.

- Explanation: As per the agile principle, welcome changing requirements, even late in development. Agile process harness change for the customer's competitive advantage. Option B is correct. Option A is not a valid agile principle. Agile naturally fit into changes are normal, and no need for a strict change control process to get approval for changing requirements. Option D relates to waterfall projects.

47. Answer: B.

- Explanation: According to the agile principle, working software is the primary measure of progress. Documentation also needed, only barely sufficient is enough. Good architecture and encouraging working environment are not valid choices. Option B is the correct answer.

48. Answer: B.

- Explanation: Option A, C, and D are the responsibilities of the product owner. Option B, which is to remove the impediments for the team is not the responsibility of the product owner. It is the responsibility of the Scrum Master.

49. Answer: D

- Explanation: In a hardening iteration, the team stops focusing on delivering new features, and instead spends their time on stabilizing the system and getting it ready to be released. Option A is for Hardening iteration. Option B, rolling wave planning is to plan the next few iterations in detail, more distant are planned at a higher level. Option C is related to Product Demo. Option D is the correct answer. Iteration Zero is an iteration where you set up all the servers, make sure we have a release plan, develop a product backlog, and in general do all those things that your project is ready to start.

50. Answer: C.

- Explanation: Option A, the team owns the process changes through the retrospective process. Scrum master supports the remove impediments for the team, and make sure the process is followed. The product owner is responsible for the changes related to the product and they represent customers. Option D is not the correct choice.

CSM (Certified Scrum Master) PRACTICE EXAM 3:

1. The timing of sprint retrospective meeting,

A. After the spring review
B. After the product review
C. After sprint review and before the next sprint planning meeting.
D. At the end of every release

2. The product backlog grooming process is led by whom?

A. The product owner
B. The team
C. XP coach
D. project manager

3. In this plan, the required features are defined first, and then the release date is calculated later.

A. Time boxed
B. Scope boxed
C. product vision box
D. product box

4. The current iteration ends, and the customer says the product didn't meet the acceptance criteria. As a scrum master, the response is

A. Add it in the next iteration backlog
B. extend the duration of the iteration

C. cancel the current iteration
D. Ignore the opinion from a customer, since the task is fixed during iteration.

5. Result of the iteration planning meeting,

A. iteration backlog
B. product backlog
C. Sprint backlog
D. risk backlog

6. Valid format of a user story,

A. Independent, negotiable, valuable, estimable, small, and testable
B. As a <user>, I want <goal>, so that <some reason>
C. <Reason> I want <goal>.
D. As a <user>, I want <goal>.

7. Not one of the Agile Manifesto

A. Working software is the primary measure of progress.
B. Customer collaboration over contract negotiation.
C. Responding to Change over following a plan.
D. Individuals and interactions over process and tools.

8. In the case of a distributed team in agile, need to consider

A. High communication bandwidth.
B. Synchronizing communication.
C. None of the above.
D. Both A and B.

9. Acronym to use for user story attributes

A. Moscow
B. DEEP
C. DRY
D. INVEST

10. A variation in the scrum, which is an enhancement, i.e. scrum with lean thinking is called

A. Lean
B. Scrum #
C. Scrum ##
D. XP.

11. One of the below options are not correct for successful agile teams,

A. Co-located.
B. Work is assigned to them.
C. Empowered.
D. Self-organizing.

12. In the scrum process definition of done is not created by one of them in the list given below

A. Product owner.
B. Scrum Master.
C. Sponsor
D. Team.

13.2 meetings team held at the end of each iteration.

A. Status meeting, Review meeting.
B. The review meeting, Retrospective meeting.
C. Team meeting, Review meeting.
D. The retrospective meeting, daily stand up meeting.

14. One of the below is not a feedback cycle in agile

A. Daily standup meeting.
B. Team meeting.
C. Iteration Review meeting.
D. Retrospective meeting.

15. One of the below is not a product owner's role

A. The single voice of the customer.
B. Prioritize the product backlog.
C. Remove the obstacles for the team.
D. It helps to define the user story, and define acceptance criteria.

16. Which Agile methodology is widely used?

A. Scrum
B. Lean
C. XP
D. Kanban

17. Who manages the iteration backlog?

A. project manager
B. the sponsor
C. the team
D. the product owner

18. How often does the entire team meet on an agile project?

A. once weekly
B. Daily
C. At the beginning of each iteration
D. Depends on the agreements between the team member and product owner

19. Estimating the effort of user stories will be represented by?

A. cycle time
B. ideal days
C. velocity
D. Calendar days

20. The number of stories that a team can deliver in an iteration is known as

A. cycle time
B. velocity
C. burn rate
D. story point

21. The activity that a team reviews its performance to improve its performance for the next iteration?

A. velocity
B. refactor
C. retrospective
D. planning poker

22. Agile Goals are defined by SMART. What does "M" mean?

A. modifiable
B. measurable
C. monetary value
D. methodology

23. The best definition of prioritization?

A. The relative ordering of user stories concerning the value
B. Always prioritize based on the priority of project manager
C. Always prioritize based on the priority of product owner

D. The team define the prioritization.

24. How does the agile team estimate the relative size of a user story?

A. using velocity
B. using story points
C. using burn rate
D. using team size

25. What is the duration of iteration?

A. one month
B. one week
C. 2 to 4 weeks
D. depends on the project

26. When a team is trusted and self-organized and makes decisions collectively it is called?

A. independent team
B. cross-functional team
C. motivated team
D. empowered team

27. In scrum methodology, which of the below serves a connection between the product owner and the team?

A. the iteration backlog
B. the product backlog
C. sprint review

D. elevator statement

28. When is the product roadmap created?

A. At the beginning of the release
B. At the beginning of the iteration
C. during the sprint review
D. At the beginning of the project

29. Your agile team is dividing user stories, into smaller, manageable tasks. What is this process called?

A. Reflection
B. WBS
C. task
D. Decomposition

30.3 levels of agile planning?

A. Daily planning, iteration planning, release planning
B. Daily standup meeting, daily planning, release planning
C. retrospective, reflective workshop, rolling wave planning
D. product backlog planning, iteration planning, release planning

31. The following is the agile feedback technique?

A. finding defect

B. prototyping
C. source code review
D. team meeting

32. Agile team members make decisions collaboratively and take ownership of a decision. The decision model is known as?

A. participatory
B. command and control
C. shared decision model
D. individual

33. The delivery which is used in agile?

A. incremental delivery
B. real time delivery
C. iteration delivery
D. functionality delivery

34. Which level of agile planning helps estimate when a product will be ready for release?

A. Project planning
B. release planning
C. sprint planning
D. iteration planning

35. The product backlog should be?

A. detailed, estimable, emergent, prioritized
B. independent, valuable, negotiable, testable

C. detailed, elegant, entertaining, prioritized
D. none of the above

36. Purpose of iteration retrospective

A. To create team ownership
B. to improve team collaboration
C. To improve future iterations
D. to meet the team

37. The current iteration ends, and the customer says the product didn't meet the acceptance criteria. As a scrum master, the response is

A. Ask for more budget and resources to complete it soon
B. Cancel the product
C. Add in the next iteration backlog
D. All of the above

38. It is a process of reviewing, adding, deleting, and re-prioritizing user stories that are considered to be important to the customer.

A. story prioritization
B. backlog grooming
C. estimation
D. sizing

39. Which is not one of the responsibilities of the product owner

A. They are responsible to write user stories
B. Remove the obstacles/impediments for the team
C. Voice of the customer and representing stakeholders and business
D. Prioritize user stories

40. One of the given options is not related to daily scrum meetings?

A. Promotes collaboration and self-organization
B. can be used as a status meeting
C. Time boxed for 15 minutes
D. Focus on goals

41. What are the tasks for the development team during the first sprint?

A. Plan the entire design and architecture
B. Develop and deliver part of the functionality of the product
C. Focus on developing initial requirement
D. All of the above

42. What are the factors to be considered for sprint length?

A. Uncertainty
B. The risk appetite of the organization
C. Length of the release

D. All of the above

43. Factors to be considered when dealing with the technical debt in a scrum project are,

A. Address technical debt during the sprint review meetings
B. All the tasks related to technical debt should be entered in the product backlog,
C. Allocate some percentage of scrum team's work for defect fixing and refactoring in every sprint
D. All of the above

44. Main causes of technical debt are

A. No proper testing during the sprint
B. complexity in design and architecture
C. Tight delivery schedule
D. All of the above

45. Some of the skill of servant leader is,

A. Remove impediments that block the progress of the project
B. empower the team
C. facilitating
D. All of the above

46. Some of the product backlog characteristics are,

A. Detailed
B. Estimable

C. Emergent
D. All of the above

47. The features of product backlog are

A. Defect fixes
B. New features to be added
C. Existing feature modifications
D. All of the above

48. The main difference between coaching and facilitation are

A. Coaching gives instructions like what to do
B. coaching focus on specific tasks, facilitation focus on the overall development
C. Facilitation helps groups or individuals to learn
D. All of the above

49. How can the scrum master help the product owner?

A. Help the product owner to arrange backlog items to maximize the value in the sprint.
B. facilitate scrum events
C. Helps the scrum team to understand backlog items
D. All of the above

50. How can the scrum master help the development team?

A. Removing impediments that block the progress
B. Coach the development team to adapt scrum practices
C. Helps development team to self-organize and cross-functional
D. All of the above

CSM PRACTICE EXAM 3: ANSWERS

1. Answer: C.

- Explanation: Sprint retrospective held after the sprint review and prior to the next sprint planning meeting. Options A, B, and D are not correct.

2. Answer: A.

- Explanation: backlog grooming is the effort led by the product owner, and supported by the team. Option A is the correct answer. It is supported by the team, scrum master, and all. Option C XP coach, Option D, Project manager are not correct choices.

3. Answer: B.

- Explanation: In a Time boxed plan, work cannot take more than the maximum amount of time defined. The product vision box contains graphic images and narrative content; notify customers what they can expect in the product. It is one of the agile tools used. There is no term called product boxed in agile. The correct answer is B. In the scope boxed plan the features are defined first, and then the release date is calculated.

4. Answer: A.

- Explanation: Once we get the feedback from customers, regarding the product didn't meet the acceptance criteria required by customers, then scrum master needs to add it in the next iteration backlog. Option B is not correct; usually, we won't extend the duration, to update the product features required by customers. Option C also not correct. The current iteration should not be canceled to accommodate the requested changes. Option D also not correct. As a scrum master, we can't say, during the fixed iteration task is fixed.

5. Answer: A.

- Explanation: The iteration backlog is the result of the iteration planning meeting. The sprint backlog is the result of a sprint planning meeting. Option D is not correct.

6. Answer: B

- Explanation: Option A is the attributes of the user story. Option B is the format of the user story. Option C and Option D are not the correct options.

7. Answer: A.

- Explanation: Option A is not an agile manifesto. It is one of the 12 agile principles.

8. Answer: D

- Explanation: Option D is the correct answer. In distributed teams, the key factors to consider are high communication bandwidth, and synchronizing communication.

9. Answer: D

A. Explanation: Attributes of a user story INVEST (independent, negotiable, valuable, estimable, small, and testable). Option A Moscow is used to prioritize user stories in agile (Must have, should have, could have, won't have). Option B DEEP is used to denote the Product backlog (It should be Detailed, Estimable, Emergent, Prioritized). DRY denotes Don't Repeat Yourself. It means don't repeat the code.

10. Answer: B

- Explanation: The correct answer is B. Scrum with lean thinking is called Scrum #. Other options are not correct.

11. Answer: B

- Explanation: Agile teams are cross-functional, co-located, and the task is not assigned to them. The agile team selects the task themselves called self-organized. And the agile team is empowered to make decisions regarding the project. Option B is like a waterfall approach. In the waterfall, the approach task is assigned to the team by the project manager. So option B is not correct for successful agile teams.

12. Answer: C

- Explanation: The definition of done is created by the entire team, scrum master, and product owner. It is a joint effort involved with everyone in the project. It is not defined by the sponsor alone. Option C is the right answer.

13. Answer: B

- Explanation: 2 meetings, team held at the end of each iteration Review meeting, and Retrospective meeting. During the review meeting potentially shippable product increment is presented to stakeholders for their review. This review meeting is a product based meeting. The retrospective meeting is process-based. In this meeting, the team identifies the ways to improve deliverables. Option B is the correct answer. Other options are not correct.

14. Answer: B

- Explanation: Daily Standup meeting is used to synchronize team member's activities. It is one of the feedback meetings related to the team. 3 questions asked in the daily standup. 1. What have you done since the last meeting? 2. What you are planning to do between now and next meeting 3. Are there any obstacles on the way? Iteration Review meeting used to happen at the end of each iteration and it is product-centric. During this meeting, customers review the product and provide their feedback. The retrospective meeting used to happen at the end of every iteration, and it is process centric. The team meeting is not the feedback cycle in agile. Option B is the correct answer.

15. Answer: C

- Explanation: The product owner is the single point of contact for customers, and helps the team to prioritize the product backlog based on customer priorities. They help to define user stories and define the acceptance criteria. Remove the obstacles for the team is not the product owner's responsibility. It is the responsibility of the scrum master. Option C is the correct answer.

16. Answer: A

- Explanation: Scrum is the most widely used methodology available in the market.

17. Answer: C

- Explanation: Items selected from the product backlog for the particular iteration. Prioritized user stories in the product backlog that the team is committed to developing during a particular iteration.

18. Answer: B.

- Explanation: The entire agile team meets daily. The team has a daily stand up meeting, which occurs daily at the same time, same place for 15 minutes to synchronize team member's activities. All other choices are not correct for the agile team.

19. Answer: B

- Explanation: Story size specified by Ideal days, actual days, story points. It is the time required to complete an activity assuming there are no interruptions so that work can be completed 100% efficiently. Cycle time is not used for estimating user stories. It is the time taken to complete the work from start to finish. Velocity is used to find the number of stories that a team can deliver within the iteration. Calendar days are also not used to estimate the effort of user stories.

20. Answer: B

- Explanation: Please refer to the previous answer explanation. The number of stories that a team can deliver within the iteration is called velocity.

21. Answer: C

- Explanation: Retrospective used for the process improvement in the teamwork. During the retrospective, the team reflects on what happened in the iteration and identifies actions for improvement going forward. Velocity is the number of stories that a team can deliver within the iteration and is not related to performance. Refactor is restructuring the code, without changing the external behavior of the code and not a performance-related review for the team. Planning poker is one of the agile technique used to estimate the story points of a user story code and is not related to the performance-related review for the team

22. Answer: B

- Explanation: Goals are defined by the acronym SMART. Specific, Measurable, Achievable, Relevant, and Time bounded. Other than B, all options are wrong.

23. Answer: A

- Explanation: Choices B, C, and D are wrong. It means the relative ordering of user stories, with respect to value.

24. Answer: B

- Explanation: The agile team estimates the relative size of a user story using story points. Velocity is defined as the number of stories that a team can deliver within the iteration. Burn rate is the cost of the agile team or the rate at which it consumes resources. Options A, C, and D are not the correct choices.

25. Answer: C

- Explanation: In general, iteration is between 2 to 4 weeks.

26. Answer: D

- Explanation: An empowered team takes ownership of a product and is collectively responsible for its delivery. Decision authority belongs to the entire team and is not related to any single individual. Cross-functional teams do not make decisions like an empowered team. An Independent team and motivated team are not the correct options.

27. Answer: B

- Explanation: The product backlog serves a connection between the product owner and the team. The iteration backlog is limited to only one iteration. The sprint review is after every sprint, to review the product. This option is not correct. Elevator statements are brief and can be shared with a fellow elevator passenger, explain the project vision in the short amount of time it takes to ride an elevator from one floor to another. This option also not correct.

28. Answer: D.

- Explanation: It is created at the beginning of the project. It is not created during the sprint review. Also, a product roadmap is not created at the beginning of the release or iteration.

29. Answer: D

- Explanation: The agile team is dividing the user stories, into smaller, manageable tasks. This process is called decomposition. Reflection is not a valid option. The task is the result of decomposition.

30. Answer: A

- Explanation: Option A is a valid level of agile planning. Other options given are not correct.

31. Answer: B

- Explanation: Prototyping is one of the agile feedback techniques for the product. The prototype is used to get valuable feedback from the users early in the project. Finding defects, source code review, and team meetings are not feedback techniques in agile.

32. Answer: A

- Explanation: The decision model where agile team members make decisions collaboratively and take ownership of the decision. This decision model is known as participatory decision making. In command and control, some individual takes the decision, not the team. Options C and D are wrong and not agile.

33. Answer: A

- Explanation: The delivery which is used in agile is incremental delivery. The product is delivered in increments in iterations. Options B, C, and D are not valid choices.

34. Answer: B

- Explanation: It is release planning. It is planned on the tactical level. Release planning to develop a project schedule, which is developed twice a year. Each Release plan contains many iterations. The roadmap contains many release plans.

35. Answer: A

- (Remember DEEP) Explanation: Product backlog should be Detailed, Estimable, Emergent, and Prioritized.

36. Answer: C

- To improve future iterations

37. Answer: C

- Add it in the next iteration backlog

38. Answer: B.

- Backlog grooming

39. Answer: C

- It is determined by the team. Both team and product owner decide what is done in the project. A list of criteria needs to be met before a product is considered to be done.
- It is not determined by the PM or the customer or the Scrum master.

40. Answer B

Option B is not correct. Daily Scrum meeting

- It is conducted for the scrum development team
- It is time-boxed for 15 minutes
- Promotes self-organization
- Promotes collaboration
- Enables transparency
- Focus on goals.

41. Answer D

- All the given options are correct. Focus on developing initial requirement, initial architecture, and setting up the environment

42. Answer: D

Below factors to be considered for the sprint length

- Risk appetite of the organization
- Length of the release
- Uncertainty

43. Answer: D

Below factors are considered when dealing the technical debt,

- Address technical debt during the sprint review meetings, so the scrum team aware of that.
- All the tasks related to technical debt should be entered in the product backlog, in that way the entire team aware of that.
- Allocate some percentage of scrum team's work for defect fixing and refactoring in every sprint

44. Answer: D

Technical debt can be caused by anyone of the below reasons,

- No proper testing during the sprint
- Complexity in design and architecture
- Tight delivery schedule
- Lack of available skills in the Scrum development team

45. Answer D

Some of the skills of a servant leader are,

- Remove impediments that block the progress of the project
- Empower the team
- Facilitating
- Mentoring and guiding the team
- Shield team from interruptions
- Communicates the project vision to the team

46. Answer: D

Product backlog characteristics should be

- Detailed
- Estimable
- Emergent
- Prioritized.

47. Answer D

Some of the features available in the product backlog are,

- Defect fixes
- New features to be added
- Existing feature modifications

48. Answer D

The difference between coaching and facilitation are,

- Coaching gives specific instructions like what to do
- Coaching focus on specific tasks, facilitation focus on the overall development
- Facilitation helps groups or individuals to learn
- Coaching follows a structured approach

49. Answer D.

The scrum master helps product owner by,

- Help product owners to arrange backlog items to maximize the value in the sprint.
- Facilitate scrum events
- Helps the scrum team to understand backlog items
- Helps the development team to understand the sprint goals

50. Answer D

The scrum master helps the development team by

- Removing impediments that block the progress
- Coach the development team to adapt scrum practices
- Helps development team to self-organize and cross-functional
- Facilitate Scrum Events

CSM (Certified Scrum Master) PRACTICE EXAM: 4

1. The scrum master helps the organization by,

A. Works with the scrum master to implement scrum practices in the organization
B. Helps the organization to understand scrum practices
C. coach the organization to adapt scrum
D. All of the above

2. One of the given options is not a valid scrum artifact. Identify that?

A. Product backlog
B. Business case
C. Sprint backlog
D. Product increment

3. Who is responsible for the definition of done in the Scrum project?

A. Scrum master
B. Product owner
C. Scrum team
D. None of the above

4. Product Backlog items have the attributes

A. Description
B. Order

C. Value
D. All of the above

5. The group decision techniques which are used in Scrum Projects?

A. Brainstorming
B. Nominal technique
C. Delphi technique
D. All of the above

6. Defined by scrum framework

A. Rules and roles
B. artifacts
C. events
D. All of the above

7. Agile team orders stories on the wall in order of effort from greatest to least is called,

A. sizing
B. burn down chart
C. Relative sizing
D. burn up chart

8. Attributes of a user story,

A. independent
B. negotiable
C. valuable
D. All of the above

9. The time required to complete an activity assuming there are no interruptions so that work can be completed 100% efficiently.

A. Ideal days
B. Actual days
C. Story Points
D. None of the above

10. Main roles of the Scrum framework?

A. Scrum master
B. Scrum team
C. Scrum product owner
D. All of the above

11. What is important in Scrum Projects?

A. Continuous improvement
B. Self-organization
C. Communication
D. All of the above

12. The maximum amount of time the sprint retrospective takes?

A. 3 hours for 30 days' sprint
B. 2 hours for 30 days' sprint
C. 1 hour for 30 days' sprint
D. 4 hours for 30 days' sprint

13. Who can change the priority of items in the product backlog at any time?

A. Project manager
B. Product owner
C. Scrum master
D. Development team

14. The sprint burndown chart is used to show

A. Total number of work hours remaining
B. Total number of tasks remaining
C. actual days
D. ideal days

15. Scrum team started working, after the first iteration the workload is more than the development team's capacity. The best action was taken by the development team?

A. Collaborate with the product owner and change items in the product backlog
B. Add additional team members to complete the sprint as per the schedule
C. Cancel the sprint
D. Work overtime to complete the sprint

16. The Process which is used for process improvements

A. Scrum
B. Kanban

C. Agile
D. XP

17. Main Scrum basics are,

A. Self-organization
B. collaboration
C. Time boxing
D. All of the above

18. Sprint consists of the following,

A. Daily scrum
B. Sprint review
C. Sprint planning
D. All of the above

19. Input to the sprint review is,

A. Sprint goal
B. Sprint backlog
C. Shippable product
D. All of the above

20. One of the options given below is not a valid agile Manifesto?

A. Comprehensive documentation over working software
B. individuals and interactions over process and tools

C. customer collaboration over contract negotiation
D. Responding to change over following a plan

21. One of the options given below is the valid agile principle. Identify that?

A. individuals and interactions over process and tools
B. working software over comprehensive documentation
C. working software is the primary measure of progress
D. Responding to change over following a plan

22. One of the options given below is not a valid agile principle. Identify that?

A. Working software is the primary measure of progress
B. Customer collaboration over contract negotiation
C. Best architectures, requirements, and designs emerge from self-organizing teams.
D. Business people and developers must work together daily throughout the project

23. Which one of these statements reflects the agile principle?

A. Projects are built around processes rather than products.
B. Projects are built around technical coding experts.
C. Projects are built around motivated individuals.
D. Projects are built around the project manager's choice.

24. Estimating the effort of user stories will be represented by?

A. Cycle time
B. Ideal days
C. Velocity
D. Calendar Days

25. How is the information Radiator helpful?

A. It is a visual representation or chart that shows project status regarding a project.
B. It tracks the number of defects in the project.
C. It displays the number of working days for a project.
D. It provides information about stakeholder locations.

26. The best definition of prioritization?

A. The relative ordering of user stories, concerning value.
B. Always prioritize, based on the priority of the project manager.
C. Always prioritize, based on the priority of the product owner.
D. The team defined the prioritization.

27. The agile estimation technique, which is used for estimating the relative work effort of large product backlog?

A. Moscow technique
B. Affinity estimating
C. 3-point estimating
D. Wideband Delphi estimating

28. Agility is the ability to balance

A. quality and quantity
B. flexibility and stability
C. cost and effort
D. triple constraints

29. Ideal team member location in agile?

A. Collocation
B. Virtual
C. Distributed
D. Global

30. One of the following is a secondary value in the agile manifesto?

A. Individuals and interactions
B. Working software
C. Customer collaboration
D. Following a plan

31. What is the optimal team size in agile?

A. 10
B. 5
C. 7 (plus or minus) 2
D. 15

32. How a scrum master initiates a scrum project in an organization, which is new to scrum?

A. Explain the necessity to adapt to scrum to stakeholders
B. identify organizational policies and changes required for policies to adapt to scrum
C. Identify & explain various techniques used to adapt to scrum
D. All of the above

33. What type of projects related to software applications to Scrum projects?

A. All types of software-related projects
B. Onsite projects

C. Offshore software projects
D. None of the above

34. Some of the challenges faced by the scrum master in the organization?

A. Distributed teams
B. Facing Resistance due to change to scrum
C. Time boxed
D. All of the above

35. Identify the situations to use scrum in the projects?

A. Requirements keep changing frequently
B. The scope is not defined
C. Process is iterative
D. All of the above

36. Do sprint activities happen in a project?

A. Sprint planning meeting decides what to develop in a sprint.
B. Product owner prioritize the requirement and update the backlog
C. The sprint backlog is developed from product backlog based on the user stories, agreed to develop in next sprint
D. All of the above

37. Spring backlog contains,

A. User stories selected from the top of the product backlog based on the capacity of the team and estimated work to be completed
B. Sprint goal
C. Plan to deliver the product during the sprint
D. All of the above

38. Kanban is a process designed to help teams work together more effectively. It is based on the principles,

A. visualize the workflow
B. limit the work in progress
C. enhance the workflow
D. all of the above

39. It is a type of information radiator. It shows the work remaining in story points or ideal days in a project. It is a graphical representation of work left for a given period. It provides a way to track the progress of the project daily. Identify the chart

A. Burn up chart
B. Burndown chart
C. Visual task board
D. Kanban board

40. In general, a sprint contains the following events

A. Sprint planning meeting
B. Daily scrum
C. Sprint review
D. All of the above

41. The following roles available in Scrum

A. product owner
B. scrum master
C. Development team
D. All of the above

42. When the sprint over in a scrum project?

A. Product owner decides to end the sprint
B. It is a time-boxed iteration. When the time is over the sprint is finished.
C. Scrum master decides to end the sprint
D. All the items in the product backlog are developed completely

43. One of the below roles in scrum is cross-functional?

A. Development team
B. Product owner
C. Scrum master
D. Project manager

44. A key stakeholder asked the scrum team to add an item to the current sprint. What is the response from the development team in this situation?

A. Remove an item from the current sprint and add this one.
B. Inform this situation to the product owner and discuss with them
C. Add the item to the current sprint
D. Add the new item to the product backlog

45. The person who has the authority to cancel the sprint?

A. Scrum development team
B. Product owner
C. Scrum master
D. Project manager

46. Identify the option given below is an opportunity to inspect and adapt?

A. Daily Scrum meeting
B. Sprint Review
C. Sprint retrospective
D. All of the above

47. It is the cost of an agile team or the rate at which it consumes resources.

A. velocity
B. burn ratio
C. burn rate
D. story points

48. It is a larger user story and can be decomposed into smaller user stories.

A. Epic
B. Scrum of Scrum
C. Backlog
D. iteration

49. When agile team members are assigned to multiple projects or assigned to a project as well as operational support. It is called

A. Fractionally distributed
B. Fractionally assigned
C. self-organization
D. Colocation

50. Difference between the product backlog and sprint backlog in Scrum?

A. There is no difference between the product backlog and sprint backlog
B. The sprint backlog is a subset of the product backlog.

C. The product backlog is the subset of the product backlog
D. None of the above

CSM PRACTICE EXAM 4: ANSWERS

1. Answer D

Scrum Master serves the organization

- Works with the scrum master to implement scrum practices in the organization
- Helps the organization to understand scrum practices
- coach the organization to adapt scrum

2. Answer B

Option B is not correct. Valid scrum artifacts are,

- Product backlog
- Sprint backlog
- Product increment

3. Answer C

The Definition of Done is created by the Scrum team

4. Answer D

Product Backlog items have the below attributes,

- Description
- Order

- Value
- Estimate

5. Answer D

Some of the group decision techniques available in scrum projects are,

- Brainstorming
- Nominal technique
- Delphi technique

6. Answer D

Defined by scrum framework,

- Rules and roles
- Artifacts
- Events

7. Answer C

- Agile team orders stories on the wall in order of effort from greatest to least is the relative sizing

8. Answer D

- Attributes of a user story
- INVEST (independent, negotiable, valuable, estimable, small, and testable).

9. Answer A

- Ideal days: Time required to complete an activity assuming there are no interruptions so that work can be completed 100% efficiently.
- Actual days: Time required to complete an activity that considers typical interruptions that result in efficiency below 100%.
- Story points: Used to quantify the work effort and complexity required to develop a user story related to other stories.

10. Answer D

- The below main roles are defined by the scrum team. Scrum product owner, Scrum Team, and Scrum Master.

11. Answer D

Things which are important in scrum projects,

- Continuous improvement
- Self-organization
- Communication

12. Answer A

- 3 hours for 30 days' sprint

13. Answer B

- The product owner can change the priority of items in the product backlog at any time

14. Answer A

- Sprint burn down chart shows the total number of work hours remaining.

15. Answer A

- Collaborate with the product owner and change items in the product backlog

16. Answer B

- Kanban: The Kanban process is mainly for process improvements. Other options are not correct.

17. Answer D

The key Scrum principles are,

- Self-organization
- Collaboration
- Time-boxing
- Iterative development

18. Answer D

Sprint consists of,

- Daily scrum
- Sprint review
- Sprint planning
- Developed work

19. Answer D

Input to the sprint review is,

- Sprint goal
- Spring backlog
- Shippable product

20. Answer A

Valid agile manifesto,

- Individuals and interactions over process and tools
- Working software over comprehensive documentation
- Customer collaboration over contract negotiation
- Responding to change over following a plan

21. Answer C

- Principe: Working software is the primary measure of progress

22. Answer B

- Customer collaboration over contract negotiation.

23. Answer: C

- Explanation: Other choices are wrong.

- In agile, Projects are built around motivated individuals in the team.

24. Answer: B

- Explanation: Story size specified by Ideal days, actual days, story points. It is the time required to complete an activity assuming there are no interruptions so that work can be completed 100% efficiently.
- Cycle time is not used for estimating user stories. It is the time taken to complete the work from start to finish.
- Velocity is used to find the number of stories that a team can deliver within the iteration. Calendar days are also not used to estimate the effort of user stories.

25. Answer: A

- Explanation: A visual representation that shows the status regarding a project. Visual display of current work status, so interested persons can get the information without disturbing the team. It has product vision, backlog, release plan, burn up, burn down chart, and working agreements.
- Information Radiator is not used to detect tracks or provide information about stakeholder location. It also won't display the number of working days for a project.

26. Answer: A

- Explanation: Choices B, C, and D are wrong. It means the relative ordering of user stories, concerning value.

27. Answer: B

- Explanation:
- Affinity estimating is an agile estimation technique, which is used for quickly estimating the relative work effort of a large number of user stories in the product backlog. User stories are arranged in a wall from small to large size depending on the efforts to develop.
- Moscow technique is a prioritization technique, not an estimation technique.
- 3-point estimating is an estimation, and is the technique that could be used to estimate a task. In a three-point estimation, 3 values are produced for every task called the best case, most likely, and worst-case estimate.
- Wideband Delphi estimating is a consensus-based estimating technique.

28. Answer: B

- Explanation: Agility is the ability to balance between flexibility and stability. All other choices are not correct.

29. Answer: A

- Explanation: The team benefits from osmotic communication by collocating its team members. Collocation is the ideal agile team location. Virtual, distributed, and global are not ideal team member's locations in agile.

30. Answer: D

- Explanation:
- Individuals and interactions over process and tools.
- Working software over comprehensive documentation.
- Customer collaboration over contract negotiation.
- Responding to Change over following a plan.
- The value on the left is more important than that on the right. Right-hand side values are secondary values.

31. Answer: C

- Explanation: It is 7 plus or minus 2.

32. Answer D

- Explain the necessity to adapt to scrum to stakeholders
- Identify organizational policies and changes required for policies to adapt to scrum

- Identify & explain various techniques used to adapt to scrum

33. Answer A.

- All types of software projects can be done through the scrum framework.

34. Answer D

Challenges faced by scrum master when the following scrum

- Distributed teams
- Facing Resistance due to change to scrum
- Time boxed

35. Answer D.

Situations to use scrum in the projects:

- Requirements keep changing frequently
- Scope is not defined
- Process is iterative

36. Answer D

- Sprint planning meeting decide what to develop in a sprint.
- Product owner prioritize the requirement and update the backlog
- Sprint backlog is developed from product backlog based on the user stories, agreed to develop in next sprint

- Team converts the user stories into tasks
- Team started working on the sprint and have a daily scrum meeting time-boxed to 15 minutes
- At the end of the sprint, the team gave a demo of the product that they developed during the sprint to the customer
- Team conduct retrospective meeting, and review the process to improve.

37. Spring backlog contains

- User stories selected from the top of the product backlog based on the capacity of the team and estimated work to be completed
- Sprint goal
- Plan to deliver the product during the sprint

38. Answer D

Kanban is a process designed to help teams work together more effectively. It is based on the principles,

- visualize the workflow
- limit the work in progress
- enhance the workflow

39. Answer B

- It is a type of information radiator. It shows the work remaining in story points or ideal days in a project. Burndown Chart is a graphical representation of work left for a given period. It provides a way to track the progress of the project daily.

40. Answer D

In general, a sprint contains the following events

- Sprint planning meeting
- Daily scrum
- Sprint review
- Sprint retrospective

41. Answer D

The following roles available in Scrum

- product owner
- scrum master
- Development team

42. Answer B

- It is a time-boxed iteration. When the time is over the sprint is finished.

43. Answer A.

- Development team role in the scrum is cross-functional

44. Answer B

- Inform this situation to the product owner and discuss with them

45. Answer B.

- The product owner has the authority to cancel the sprint.

46. Answer D

Opportunity to inspect and adapt

- Daily Scrum meeting
- Sprint Review
- Sprint retrospective

47. Answer C

- It is the cost of an agile team or the rate at which it consumes resources.

48. Answer A

- Epic span around many iterations called a capacity. It is the larger part of the user story. Epic is a larger user story and can be decomposed into smaller user stories.

49. Answer B

- When agile team members are assigned to multiple projects or assigned to the project as well as operational support. Agile project managers avoid them and have resources assigned to only one project at a time.

50. Answer B

- The sprint backlog is a subset of the product backlog

CSM (Certified Scrum Master) PRACTICE EXAM: 5

1. Provide an example of how a Scrum Team will inspect and adapt and increase transparency at each of the Scrum events?

A. The purpose of being transparent in the scrum project is, it will create trust and bring the stakeholders together.

B· Also being transparent it is easy to communicate and provide feedback in both the directions without any hesitation in the scrum ceremonies.

C. Options A and B are correct

D. Only Option A is correct.

2. Some of the Scrum development team responsibilities are,

A. · Execute the sprint as per the plan and test the product backlog items

B· Deliver the potentially releasable increment of "done" at the end of every sprint

C· Help product owner/scrum master to prioritize user stories in product backlog during the sprint planning meeting

D. All of the above

3. Product Owner responsibilities during sprint planning meetings are?

A. The product owner explains the product backlog items to the scrum development team during the sprint planning meeting.

B. The product owner explains the team the highest priority items in the backlog in the sprint planning meeting.

C. Both A and B are correct

D. Only Option B is correct

4. Scrum Master Role during the Sprint Planning Meeting is?

A. Scrum master facilitates the sprint planning meeting.

B. Scrum Master makes sure agreements are reached in the sprint goal and the agreed product backlog items are included in the sprint backlog.

C. Both A and B are correct

D. Only Option B is correct

5. Identify some of the Development team responsibilities in daily scrum meetings are?

A· the scrum development team participates in the daily standup meeting.

B· Development team talks about the progress toward the spring goal, and any obstacles are in their way to reach the goal.

C· Scrum development team reviews the common sprint goal and its progress in the meeting.

D. All of the above

6. Sam is the product owner representing the customer. He is involved with the Scrum development team in a project. Some of the Product owner responsibilities in daily scrum meeting are,

A. The product owner can join the meeting and listen and observe, but won't interact

B. The product owner has no active role in the meeting.

C. Both Option A and B are correct

D. only Option A is correct

7. Jessica is working as a Scrum Master in the company that is leading software provider in the North America region. Some of her roles as a Scrum master role in daily scrum meeting are,

A· Scrum master keeps the daily scrum within the specified 15-minute duration.

B· Daily scrum meeting is mainly conducted for the development team. Others can participate in the meeting. Scrum Master ensures that other participants are not interrupting the meeting

C. Both Option A and B are correct

D. Only Option B is correct

8. Samantha is working as a lead developer in the Scrum Development team. The role of the Scrum development team in the sprint review meeting is,

A· during sprint review the actual increment is reviewed.

B· Development team reviews what went well in the sprint, and what impediments they faced during the sprint, and how they resolve the impediments.

C· the product increment is validated against the spring goal that was planned in the sprint planning meeting.

D. All of the above

9. Richard is working as a product owner in a Scrum project. The company that Richard is working for is a leading automobile company in the South America

region. Some of Richard's role as a Product Owner in the sprint review meeting is,

A· Product owner conducts the sprint review meeting and compares the product increments with the sprint goal that was planned in the sprint planning meeting.

B· Product owner and other stakeholders review the product increment and compares against what was planned and what was accomplished during the sprint.

C. Both Option A and B are correct

D. Only Option A is correct

10. Lisa is working as a Scrum master in a leading airline company in the North America region. Some of her roles as a Scrum Master in sprint review meeting are,

A· Scrum master arranges the sprint review meeting immediately after the sprint.

B· Scrum master enforces the timeframe for the meeting.

C. Both Option A and B are correct

D. Option A is correct

11. Techcorp INC is the leading Robotics Company in the North America region. Anthony is working as a

Scrum Master in a time-sensitive project. Some of his roles as a Scrum Master in the retrospective are,

A· Scrum master is the facilitator in the retrospective meeting.

B· Issues are discussed in the retrospective, and scrum master makes sure it is addressed by the development team before the next sprint.

C. Both Option A and B are correct

D. Only Option A is correct

12. Rebecca is working as a product owner in a leading Real Estate company in the European region. The project that Rebecca is working on has a tight budget. Some of Rebecca's roles as a Product Owner in retrospective

A· Product owner participates in the retrospective to increase collaboration between them and the development team.

B. Scrum master and product owner can participate in the meeting.

C. Both Option A and B are correct

D. Only Option A is correct

13. Explain the reasons why the Sprint Goal does not change during a Sprint?

A· Development team commits to meet the goal at the end of the sprint, and the product owner commits not to change the sprint goal during the sprint.

B· Sprint goal is the mutual commitment between the scrum development team and the product owner. If the goal is changed then the scope of the sprint will be changed, and the development team cannot complete the sprint on time.

C. Both Option A and B are correct

D. Only Option A is correct

14. Describe the outcome of every Sprint?

A· every sprint must have one goal.

B· the goal is defined before the start of the sprint.

C· Sprint goal is achieved through the implementation of product backlog items.

D. All of the above

15. Energy Efficient INC is the leading energy provider in the United Kingdom. Emma is working as a product owner in the company for the last 10 years. Some of

the Activities of Emma as a product owner during sprint planning meeting are,

A· product owner represents the customer during the sprint planning meeting.

B· Product owner and the development team jointly develop the objective of the upcoming sprint.

C· during the sprint planning meeting Product owner explains the features developed during the next sprint and the development team clarifies all the doubts from the product owner.

D. All of the above

16. Scott is working for a Scrum project as a senior software developer in the development team. Some of the activities of the development team during sprint planning meeting are,

A· in the spring planning meeting, the scrum development team establishes the goals for the next sprint along with the product owner and scrum master.

B· during the first session the Product Owner presents the highest priorities of the Product Backlog to the team. The highest priority items from the backlog, the development team agrees to develop for the upcoming next sprint.

C· Development team decomposes the high-level user story defined by the product owner in the product backlog into detailed tasks for the sprint backlog.

D. All of the above

17. How to write a sprint goal in a Scrum project?

A· Sprint goals should be SMART (specific, measurable, attainable, relevant and time-bounded)

B· In general goal is written as 1 to 2 sentences and describes what is going to be developed by the scrum development team in the upcoming sprint.

C · It is developed by negotiation between the development team and product owner and it is developed collaboratively.

D. All of the above

18. Samantha is working on a Scrum project as a team member. She participates regularly in the daily scrum meeting. Does daily scrum meetings differ from a status meeting?

A. Daily Scrum meeting is conducted for the development team to synchronize the development of team activities.

B. It helps the development team to self-organize and empowered to make their own decisions.

C. Both Option A and B are correct

D. Option A is correct.

19. Patrick is working as a Scrum Master in a leading Telecom company in the South Africa region. Patrick is working with the product owner and the development of the recent project. Some of the activities that occur during the Sprint Review meeting are,

A· Development team discusses the increment they developed during the sprint and further they explain what went well, what the impediments they faced are, and how they resolve the issues.

B· Product increment is assessed against what was originally planned in the sprint planning meeting.

C. The product owner discusses the work done in the product backlog and the work not done from the product backlog.

D. All of the above

20. Brandon is the product owner in a leading aeronautical company in the South America region. He along with the Scrum master and the scrum development team participates in the Sprint Review meeting. Some of the Potential outcomes for a Sprint Review meeting are,

A· One of the outcomes of the sprint review meeting is revised product backlog items, which is going to be developed in the next sprint.

B· the product backlog is adjusted against the new risks and opportunities.

C. Both Option A and B are correct

D. Only Option A is correct

21. Gloria is working as a Scrum master in a leading Insurance company in India. Gloria along with the product owner and the Scrum development team participated in the Sprint Retrospective meeting. The Approaches related to conducting a Sprint Retrospective meeting,

A· Sprint retrospective occurs after the sprint review but before the next sprint planning.

B· in the meeting discuss what went well during the sprint, and what went not well and how to improve the process.

C. Option A is correct

D. Both Option A and B are correct

22. Ralph is working as a Scrum master in a fortune 500 company. Ralph and the Scrum development team is working on the product backlog. Some of the Attributes of a Product Backlog item are,

A.product description,

B. the definition of done

C. Work to be completed,

D. All of the above

23. Judy is a product owner in a Scrum project. Most of the time Judy works with the Scrum development team related to the Sprint Backlog. Currently, Judy is working with the Scrum development team to finalize the Sprint Backlog. The Essential characteristics of the Sprint Backlog are,

A· Sprint backlog contains high priority user stories from the product backlog.

B· Exhibits the characteristics DEEP (detailed, estimable, emergent and prioritized)

C. Both Option A and B are correct

D. Only Option A is correct

24. Bradley is working as a Scrum Master in the company. The company that Bradley is working is the leading electronic products distribution company in Canada. The product owner wanted to add new features to the Sprint Backlog. How the Sprint Backlog can be changed without endangering the Sprint Goal?

A· Sprint backlog only can be updated by the scrum development team. They update the backlog with completed work and the remaining work.

B. If needed eliminate added work in the backlog and add the new work to the backlog. This can be only done by the development team.

C. Both Option A and B are correct

D. Only Option B is correct

25. Sophia is working as a Scrum Master in a leading Healthcare company in the North America region. She worked with the Scrum development team and the Scrum Master in the current sprint. She always enforces the strong definition of done for the user stories. Identify the Importance of a strong definition of done in Scrum?

A· If the definition of done is done correctly it will avoid rework, waste.

B· One of the advantages of the definition of done is correctly, then the chances of acceptance of the product by the product owner/customer are more.

C· by having a strong definition of done, prevent the lower quality products or product increments handed over to the customer.

D. All of the above

26. Vincent is working as a Scrum Master in a leading logistics company in the North America region. He worked with the Scrum development team and the Scrum Master in the current sprint. She always enforces the strong definition of done for the user stories. Identify the risks associated with a weaker definition of done scrum?

A· the definition of done should be defined correctly. Weaker definition of done results in customer dissatisfaction, risks, and delays.

B· Weaker definition of done results in the chances of acceptance of the product by the product owner/customer is less.

C· Weaker definition of done results in partial product working, and part of increment is not working.

D. All of the above.

27. Marie is working as a Scrum Master in the organization for the last couple of years. She is working with the Scrum development team and product owner to finalize the definition of done. Identify the correct option related to the Definition of done from the given options?

A· Definition of done is created by the scrum development team.

B. Acceptance criteria in the definition of done are created by the product owner.

C· When the product increment met the acceptance criteria in the definition of done, the product will be accepted by the customer/product owner.

D. All of the above

28. Douglas is working as a Scrum Master in a leading financial company in Mexico. Due to the complexity and amount of the work of the new project multiple teams working on the same product backlog. Identify the reasons why multiple teams working on the same Product Backlog have a shared and consistent definition of "Done."?

A· If the project is very big in size, sometimes it is executed by multiple scrum development teams. If multiple teams are working on the product, then all the teams mutually define the definition of done for the product.

B· Even though it is mutually defined by all the scrum teams, every team maintains its own product backlog.

C. Both Option A and B are correct

D. Only Option A is correct

29. Victoria is working as a Scrum Master in a leading transport corporation in the Australia region. She used to work with the Scrum Development team and product owner. Some of the Scrum Master Core Competencies are,

A· they facilitate meetings daily scrum meetings, sprint planning meetings, sprint review, and sprint retrospective.

B· Shield the team from interruptions

C· Remove impediments

D. All of the above

30. Joyce is working as a Scrum Master in a leading Pharmaceutical company in Europe. She worked with the Scrum development team and the Scrum Master in the current sprint. Identify how Joyce as a Scrum Master helps the scrum team by facilitation?

A· Scrum master helps the scrum team by facilitating scrum events like sprint planning, daily scrum meeting, and scrum review and sprint retrospectives.

B· Scrum master facilitates the development team in delivering the product increment by ensuring the team follows the Scrum practices.

C. Both Option A and B are correct

D. Only Option B is correct

31. Walter is working as a Scrum Master in a leading Energy company in the South America region. He is working with the Scrum development team and the Scrum Master in the current sprint. Walter suggests some Scrum techniques for facilitating group decision making. Identity the facilitation techniques that are used for group decision making in Scrum?

A. Nominal group technique

B. Delphi technique

C. brainstorming

D. All of the above

32. Ralph is working as a Scrum Master in a leading chain grocery in the Singapore region. He is working with the Scrum development team and the product owner in the current sprint. He suggests the nominal

group technique for group decision making. Identify the nominal group decision-making technique from the given options?

A. This technique is used to get the opinions of experts. In this technique, instead of everybody in the same room, the questionnaire is sent to risk experts and asking about the risks in the project. Once the questionnaire is collected, it was recirculated again to reach the consensus in opinion. It will take a few rounds to reach the consensus. In this technique, nobody knows about who else is involved in this process.

B. It is derived from a brainstorming technique. It involves a voting process to rank the ideas generated. The ideas which have more votes will be selected as the result of the session. In this technique, ideas are generated using brainstorming in a small group environment and then reviewed by a larger group.

C. It is a group creativity technique by which efforts are made to find a conclusion for a specific problem by gathering a list of ideas spontaneously contributed by its members.

D. All of the above

33. Kelly is working as a Scrum Master in a leading Branding company in the Switzerland region. She is working with the Scrum development team and the product owner in the current sprint. She suggests the Delphi technique for group decision making. Identify the Delphi technique from the given options?

A. This technique is used to get the opinions of experts. In this technique, instead of everybody in the same room, the questionnaire is sent to risk experts and asking about the risks in the project. Once the questionnaire is collected, it was recirculated again to reach the consensus in opinion. It will take a few rounds to reach the consensus. In this technique, nobody knows about who else is involved in this process.

B. It is derived from a brainstorming technique. It involves a voting process to rank the ideas generated. The ideas which have more votes will be selected as the result of the session. In this technique, ideas are generated using brainstorming in a small group environment and then reviewed by a larger group.

C. It is a group creativity technique by which efforts are made to find a conclusion for a specific problem by gathering a list of ideas spontaneously contributed by its members.

D. All of the above

34. Scott is working as a Scrum Master in a leading chain grocery in the South Africa region. He is working with the Scrum development team and the product owner in the current sprint. He suggests the Brainstorming technique for group decision making. Identify the Brainstorming technique from the given options?

A. This technique is used to get the opinions of experts. In this technique, instead of everybody in the same room, the questionnaire is sent to risk experts and asking about the risks in the project. Once the questionnaire is collected, it was recirculated again to reach the consensus in opinion. It will take a few rounds to reach the consensus. In this technique, nobody knows about who else is involved in this process.

B. It is derived from a brainstorming technique. It involves a voting process to rank the ideas generated. The ideas which have more votes will be selected as the result of the session. In this technique, ideas are generated using brainstorming in a small group environment and then reviewed by a larger group.

C. It is a group creativity technique by which efforts are made to find a conclusion for a specific problem by gathering a list of ideas spontaneously contributed by its members.

D. All of the above

35. Innovation First INC is the leading technology company in Mexico. Mathew is the Scrum master working for the company for the last 5 years. Mathew had a discussion in one of the meeting about the difference between coaching and facilitation. Identify the difference between coaching and facilitation. A. Scrum master facilitates the sprint planning meeting.

A· Coaching is more directive in nature than the facilitation

B· Facilitation helps the groups as well as the individual teams

C· both coaching and facilitation helps the team to improve the performance

D. All of the above

36. Grace is working as a Scrum Master in a leading Healthcare company in the Switzerland region. She worked with the Scrum development team and the Scrum Master in the current sprint. She always prefers to work as a Servant-leader for the team. How does a Scrum Master serve as a Servant-Leader in the organization?

A· Shield the team from interruptions

B· Coach the team regarding the self-organization

C· Coaching the team in adopting scrum in the organization

D. All of the above

37. Network Services INC is a leading Sports Programming Network company in Canada. Madison is working as a Scrum Master in the company for the last few years. She worked with the Scrum development team and the Scrum Master in the current sprint. Identify the Scenarios where the Scrum Master acts as the servant-leader for the Development Team?

A· Remove impediments for the scrum team

B· Coach the team regarding the self-organization, and not telling them what to do

C. Both Option A and B are correct

D. Only Option A is correct

Answer: Option C is correct.

38. Sophia is working as a Scrum Master in a leading Healthcare company in the North America region. She worked with the Scrum development team and the Scrum Master in the current sprint. She always enforces the strong definition of done for the user stories. Identify the Importance of a strong definition of done in Scrum?

A· Scrum development teamwork may be disturbed by the product owner or other key stakeholders in the project. Scrum Master makes sure it won't happen in their project.

B· some of the user stories in the product backlog are kept without the proper acceptance criteria.

C. Both Option A and B are correct

D. Only Option B is correct

39. Qual Food Corporation is a leading Food processing company in Mexico. Jason is working as a Scrum Master in the company for the last few years. He is working with the Scrum development team and the Scrum Master in the current sprint. Identify the development practices that will help Scrum Teams deliver a high-quality Product Increment and reduce technical debt each Sprint?

A· the tasks related to technical debt must be entered into the product backlog so that the scrum team is aware of that.

B· Always allocate some percentage of tasks to deal with the defect fixing.

C. Both Option A and B are correct

D. Only Option A is correct

40. Energy First Corporation is a leading Energy drink company in Europe. Ariana is working as a Scrum Master in the company for the last few years. She is working with the Scrum development team and the Scrum Master in the current sprint. How Ariana as a Scrum Master helps Product Owner in the project?

A· Work closely with the product owner and keep the product backlog updated for the upcoming sprints.

B· Scrum master helps the product owner and the scrum development team to follow the correct processes and agile principles and help them to choose the correct tools & techniques

C. Options A and B are correct

D. Only Option B is correct

41. Reliable Communication is a leading Telecom provider in Asia. Greyson is working as a Scrum Master in the company for the last few years. He is working with the Scrum development team and the Scrum Master in the current sprint. John is the product owner of the current project. Identify the reason that Product Owner participates in the Sprint Retrospective?

A· Product owner participates in the retrospective to increase collaboration between them and the development team.

B· Retrospectives are mainly for the scrum development team. Scrum master and product owner can participate in the meeting.

C. Options A and B are correct

D. Option B is correct

42. All Brands Corporation is a leading consumer goods company in Malaysia. Ivy is working as a Scrum Master in the company for the last few years. She is working with the Scrum development team and the Scrum Master in the current sprint. John is the product owner of the current project. Identify the ways that the Scrum Master assists the Scrum Team with impediments?

A· Remove impediments for the scrum team. Sometimes scrum team will remove the impediments on their own. In case if they are not able to remove the impediments then the scrum master helps to remove it.

B· Scrum master adds the impediments in the product backlog and works with the development team to remove the impediments.

C. Both Option A and B are correct

D. Only Option B is correct

43. All Circuit is a leading consumer electronics company in the United Kingdom. Mason is working as a Scrum Master in the company for the last few years. He is working with the Scrum development team and the Scrum Master in the current sprint. Randy is the product owner of the current project. Mason is working on identifying the organizational impediments that are going to affect the current sprint. Identify the 3 organizational impediments that can affect Scrum Teams?

A· Organizational culture

B· Lack of training or knowledge by the team

C· Organizational and technical impediments

D. All of the above

44. High-Grade Oil is a leading oil company in the Middle East region. Robert is working as a Scrum Master in the company for the last few years. He is working with the Scrum development team and the Scrum Master in the current sprint. Valentina is the product owner of the current project. Identify the example of an organizational design change caused by adopting Scrum?

A· Teams can be cross-functional

B· Departments can be merged into a single department based on the product group.

C. Both Option A and B are correct

45. Grocery first is a leading grocery company in South Africa. Madeline is working as a Scrum Master in the company for the last few years. She is working with the Scrum development team and the Scrum Master in the current sprint. Joseph is the product owner of the current project. Identify the reason why the Scrum project does not have a project manager?

A· Scrum only defines 3 roles Scrum Master, Product Owner, and development team

B· Project manager is outside of the scrum team, and there is no role as project manager defined in scrum projects

C. Options A and B are correct

D. Only Option A is correct

46. Cruise Unlimited is a leading cruise company in Alaska. Aurora is working as a Scrum Master in the company for the last few years. She is working with the Scrum development team and the Scrum Master in the current sprint. Ralph is the product owner of the current project. Identify the Definition of Scrum from the given definitions?

A· Scrum is a framework for agile software development.

B· Scrum projects progress through a series of iterations called sprints.

C. Both Options A and B are correct

D. Option B is correct

47. Andrew is working as a Scrum Master in a leading energy provider company in the North America region. He worked with the Scrum development team and the Scrum Master in the current sprint. Mark is the product owner of the project. When working in an iteration review meeting they had a discussion related to the Relationship of Scrum to Agile process. Identify the relationship between the Scrum to Agile?

A· Agile describes a set of guiding principles that uses an iterative approach for software development

B· Scrum is a specific set of rules that are to be followed while practicing the agile software development

C. Both Option A and B are correct

D. Option D is correct

48. Michael is working as a Scrum Master in a leading software provider company in the South America region. He worked with the Scrum development team and the Scrum Master in the current sprint. Earl is the product owner of the project. When working in an iteration review meeting they had a discussion related to the Empirical process control as it relates to scrum. Identify the empirical process control related to Scrum?

A· In Scrum, an empirical process is implemented where progress is based on observation and experimentation instead of detailed, upfront planning and defined processes.

B· Empirical process relies on the three main ideas of transparency, inspection, and adaptation

C. Both Option A and B are correct

D. Only Option B is correct

49. Samuel is working as a Scrum Master in a leading robotics company in the Philippines region. He worked with the Scrum development team and the Scrum Master in the current sprint. Amanda is the product owner of the current project. Samuel is a big fan of incremental delivery in iterations. Identify how and why "incremental" is an important characteristic of scrum?

A· Scrum is incremental because work is delivered throughout the project at regular intervals through iterations

B· Instead of getting the feedback at the end of the final product, the feedback is obtained for every increment. This helps the team to make changes early and often.

C. Both Option A and B are correct

D. Only Option A is correct

50. Stella is working as a Scrum Master in a leading AI company in the Australia region. He worked with the Scrum development team and the Scrum Master in the current sprint. Identify the Applicability of Scrum in the projects?

A. Scrum is also applicable to any projects with tight timelines, complex requirements, and requirements are not known at the beginning of the project

B. Scrum is an agile process used only in software industries and artificial intelligence projects

C. Both Option A and B are correct

D. Only Option A is correct

51. Audrey is working as a Scrum Master in a Fashion company in the Paris region. She worked with the Scrum development team and the Scrum Master in the current sprint. From the given options identify the core scrum values?

A. Commitment

B. Focus

C. Openness

D. All of the above

52. Eva is working as a Scrum Master in a leading Education provider company in the Middle East region. She is working with the Scrum development team and the Scrum Master in the current sprint. One of her meeting she explains about the importance of commitment in the Scrum projects. Identify how and why commitment is an important Scrum value?

A· Development team commits in the scrum project by creating an increment according to the definition of done

B· Scrum master shows commitment to the project by not extending the duration of the sprint, also commit to removing the impediments that can't be handled by the development team

C. Both Option A and B are Correct

D. Option B is correct

53. Infinite Media is a leading media production company in New Zealand. Ruby is working as a Scrum Master in the company for the last few years. She is working with the Scrum development team and the Scrum Master in the current sprint. Randy is the product owner of the current project. Identify how and why courage is an important Scrum value in scrum projects?

A· Scrum Development team has the courage to ask for help and to take calculated risks in the project

B. Scrum Master has the courage to remove impediments that block the team's progress and also stop the last minute's changes introduced in the sprint.

C. Option B is correct

D. Both Option A and B are correct

54. Trends is a leading Semiconductor company in Italy. Anthony is working as a Scrum Master in the company for the last few years. He is working with the Scrum development team and the Scrum Master in the current sprint. Murphy is the product owner of the current project. Identify how and why focus is an important Scrum value in scrum projects?

A· Scrum team focus on only the work to be done in a sprint by limiting the work in progress that eliminates waste

B· Scrum team focus on delivering the increment as per the definition of done at the end of every sprint

C· Scrum master allows the team to focus and define their own definition of done

D. All of the above

55. Fast Shipping Corporation is a leading Shipping company in the Netherlands. Kaylee is working as a Scrum Master in the company for the last few years. She is working with the Scrum development team and the Scrum Master in the current sprint. Bob is the product owner of the current project. Identify how and why openness is an important Scrum value in scrum projects?

A· Openness supports transparency

B· Openness allows the scrum team to share their opinions openly and heard by the teams.

C· Openness allows the team to allow the team if they are done anything wrong and able the team to correct from their mistakes

D. All of the above

56. Retail First corporation is the leading retailing company in Britain. Rebecca is the Scrum master working for the company for the last 5 years. Rebecca had a discussion in one of the meetings about the self-organization. Identify the invalid characteristic of self-organizing from the given options?

A· the members of the team has diverse experience, skills which is essential to complete the project successfully

B· in scrum self-organization promotes shared ownership.

B· in scrum self-organization promotes shared ownership.

D· Increase the motivation of the scrum team

57. Welcome Mart Corporation is the leading Food Market Company in Brazil. Gloria is the Scrum master working for the company for the last 10 years. Gloria had a discussion in one of the meetings about the cross-functional team characteristics. Identify the invalid characteristic of the cross-functional Scrum team from the given options?

A· Cross-functional team has all skills necessary to accomplish the product without depending on other teams that are not part of the scrum team.

B. It Increases the chances of team buy-in

C· the members of the team has diverse experience, skills which is essential to complete the project successfully

D· It increases the creativity and problem-solving skills of the team members.

58. Affordable Construction is the leading construction company in the Netherlands. Gerald is the Scrum master working for the company for the last 10 years. Gerald had a discussion in one of the meetings about the main roles of the Scrum team. Identify the invalid Scrum role from the given options?

A. Product Owner

B. Scrum Master

C. Project Manager

D. Scrum Development team

59. Reliable Insurance is the leading insurance company in Germany. Kayla is the Scrum master working for the company for the last 10 years. Kayla had a discussion in one of the meetings about the main responsibilities of the Scrum Master. Identify the invalid responsibilities of Scrum Master from the given options?

A· Remove impediments for the scrum team

B. · Convey the needs of the stakeholders to the development team to develop the right product

C· Protect the team from distractions

D· Coach/mentor to the scrum team

60. Service First is the leading Utility Company in Australia. Jeremy is the Scrum master working for the company for the last 10 years. Kayla had a discussion in one of the meetings about the main characteristics of the Scrum Master. Identify the invalid characteristics of Scrum Master from the given options?

A· Facilitate scrum ceremonies

B· Coach agile practices to the team

C· Responsible to define and prioritize user stories in the product backlog

D· Create the environment that communication is smooth between the scrum team and product owner

61. Media Enterprise is the leading Media Company in Japan. Martha is the Scrum master working for the company for the last 15 years. Kayla had a discussion in one of the meetings about the main responsibilities of the product owner. Identify the invalid

responsibilities of Scrum Product owner from the given options?

A· The product owner is responsible for product vision and responsible for prioritizing and reprioritizing product backlog.

B· Teaching Scrum and seeing that it is adopted and used correctly.

C· Prioritize the items in the product backlog

D. Responsible to define the user stories in the product backlog

62. Quality Services is the leading Business Services & Supply Company in the South America region. Keith is the Scrum master working for the company for the last 20years. Keith had a discussion in one of the meetings about the main characteristics of the product owner. Identify the invalid Characteristics of Scrum Product owner from the given options?

A· they should be available when needed by the development team

B· Convey the needs of the stakeholders to the development team to develop the right product

C· Facilitate scrum ceremonies

D· Responsible to define and prioritize user stories in the product backlog

63. Comfort stay is the leading Hotel chain in the Singapore region. Megan is the Scrum master working for the company for the last 3 years. Megan had a discussion in one of the meetings about the scrum team responsibilities. Identify the invalid Characteristics of the Scrum development team from the given options?

A· Develop the product backlog items into increments of potentially shippable functionality as agreed during the sprint

B· Work with the product owner and scrum master in the sprint planning meeting to prioritize the product backlog items

C· Remove impediments for the scrum team

D· Develop the product as per the definition of done

64. Fast Trans is the leading Transportation Company in Europe. Ethan is the Scrum master working for the company for the last 3 years. Ethan had a discussion in one of the meetings about the scrum development team characteristics. Identify the invalid characteristics of the Scrum development team from the given options?

A· Development team is cross-functional

B· Convey the needs of the stakeholders to the development team to develop the right product

C· they are self-organizing

D· No sub-teams in the development team, the team members have all the necessary skills to develop the product

65. Trans First is the leading Telecom hardware manufacturing company located in Paris. Sharon is the Scrum master working for the company for the last few years. Sharon had a discussion in one of the meetings about the role of Scrum master as a servant-leader for the Scrum development team. Identify the invalid characteristics of the Scrum Master role as a servant-leader for the Scrum development team from the given options?

A· they coach the team to follow agile/Scrum principles

B· they answer questions related to the product requirements to the development team. They can decide whether to accept or reject the project.

C· they remove impediments for the team

D. · Focus on the needs of the team members with the goal of achieving results aligned with organizational goals.

66. Reliable Auto is the leading Telecom Automotive Company located in Mexico. Aaron is the Scrum master working for the company for the last few years. Aaron had a discussion in one of the meetings about the services of Scrum master to the organization. Identify the wrong option related to the Scrum Master Service to the organization from the given options?

A· Coach the scrum team and organization to follow scrum practices

B· Help the team to create product increment and remove the impediments for the team

C. · Develop the product as per the definition of done

D· Work with the product owner related to the product backlog and make sure it is ready for the next sprint

67. All Organic is the leading Food Distribution Company located in Brazil. Janet is the Scrum master working for the company for the last few years. Janet had a discussion in one of the meetings about the characteristics of the sprint. Identify the invalid option related to the characteristics of the sprint from given options?

A· at the beginning of the sprint, the goals are defined.

B· at the end of the sprint entire team with the product owner review the developed product during the sprint, and if variations are found then the adjustments are made.

C. It contains the set of features, fixes, bugs or any other activities that a development team will deliver in the upcoming iterations

D· Scrum team works towards the goal during the sprint

68. Quality Paper is the leading paper company located in Canada. Julie is the Scrum master working for the company for the last few years. Julie had a discussion in one of the meetings about the purpose of the sprint. Identify the invalid option related to the purpose of the sprint from the given options?

A· every sprint starts with a sprint review meeting and ends with a sprint planning

B· Sprint is a time-boxed iteration and the agreed work is completed during the sprint

C· Scrum development team delivers the increment of functionality at every sprint

D· Deliver the increment of the product as per the definition of done is the main purpose of the sprint

69. XYX corporation is the leading construction company located in Germany. Dennis is the Scrum master working for the company for the last few years. Dennis had a discussion in one of the meetings about the characteristics of the sprint planning in Scrum. Identify the invalid option related to characteristics of the sprint planning in Scrum from the given options?

A· every sprint has a sprint planning meeting which happens at the beginning of the sprint

B· Sprint planning meeting is attended by the scrum development team, product owner and the scrum master

C· Result of the sprint planning meeting is product backlog and product roadmap that the team agreed

D· the development team is in agreement with the product owner that they develop the specific features as defined in the backlog

70. RA Corporation is the leading retail company located in the South Africa region. Doris is the Scrum master working for the company for the last few years. Doris had a discussion in one of the meetings about the participant's role in the sprint planning meeting in Scrum. Identify the participant's role which is invalid in the sprint planning meeting from the given options?

A· Development team defines the sprint goal along with the product owner. Pick the sprint backlog items from the product backlog

B· Scrum Master explains the backlog and defines the highest priority items in the backlog. Also, they define the sprint goal along with the sprint development team

C· Scrum master facilitates the sprint planning meeting

D. None of the above

71. Reliable Utilities is the leading utility company located in India. Samy is the Scrum master working for the company for the last few years. Samy had a discussion in one of the meetings about the purpose of the sprint planning meeting in Scrum. Identify the purpose of the sprint planning meeting from the given options?

A. Development team determines the product backlog items they will deliver during the sprint

B. Define the increment that is going to be delivered in the upcoming sprint, and how the team is going to deliver

C. Both Option A and B are correct

D. Only Option A is correct

72. Affordable Package is the leading package company located in South America. Janice is the Scrum master working for the company for the last few years. Janice had a discussion in one of the meetings about the Characteristics of daily standup meetings in the scrum. Identify the invalid Characteristics of daily standup meetings in the scrum from the given options?

A· they discuss the user stories developed and the impediments for their work

B· It is conducted mostly for the Scrum Master to synchronize their activities and improve the communication between the customer.

C· Daily standup meeting is time-boxed and it happens at the same place and at the same time

D· It is the short meeting has a duration of 15 minutes

73. Strong Steel Corporation is the leading steel manufacturing company located in the Middle East. Bryan is the Scrum master working for the company for the last few years. Bryan had a discussion in one of the meetings about the Value of daily standup meetings in the scrum. Identify the Value of daily standup meetings in the scrum from the given options?

A· this is conducted for the development team and the team discuss the user stories that they developed, not developed and if there are any impediments on their way

B· It helps the communication between the team members, and identify the impediments that stop their work

C. Both Option A and B are correct

D. Only Option A is correct

74. Rental anywhere is the leading Auto Retailer Company located in the Asia region. Alexis is the Scrum master working for the company for the last few years. Alexis had a discussion in one of the meetings about the Role of participants in daily standup meetings in the scrum. Identify the invalid daily standup meeting's role in the scrum from the given options?

A· this is conducted for the development team and the team discuss the user stories that they developed, not developed and if there are any impediments on their way

B· Project Manager Coaches the team to keep the daily standup meeting within 15 minutes duration

C· If other stakeholders participate, they should not interrupt the meeting.

D· Scrum master and product owner also attend the meeting

75. Agri Equip is the leading Agriculture equipment company located in the Malaysia region. Randy is the Scrum master working for the company for the last few years. Randy had a discussion in one of the meetings about the Characteristics of a sprint review meeting. Identify the invalid Characteristics of a sprint review meeting from the given options?

A. Development team explains about the product and discuss what went well and what not went well during the sprint and the obstacles they faced

B. It is held after the sprint planning meeting

C. It is conducted to inspect the product features developed during the sprint

D. It is held at the end of the sprint

76. Med Device Corporation is the leading Medical devices company located in the Canada region. Angela is the Scrum master working for the company for the last few years. Angela had a discussion in one of the meetings about the role of participants in the sprint

review meeting. Identify the invalid participant role in the sprint review meeting from the given options?

A· Product owner and other stakeholders review the product increment and compares against what was planned and what was accomplished during the sprint.

B· Scrum Master gave a demo about the product that is developed in the sprint.

C· Scrum master arranges the sprint review meeting immediately after the sprint.

D· Product owner conducts the sprint review meeting and compares the product increments with the sprint goal that was planned in the sprint planning meeting.

77. Bio Research Corporation is the leading biotechnology company located in the European region. Scott is the Scrum master working for the company for the last few years. Scott had a discussion in one of the meetings about the Characteristics of the retrospective meeting. Identify the invalid Characteristics of the retrospective meeting from the given options?

A. It is mainly conducted to inspect the product features developed during the sprint

B· the retrospective meeting used to happen at the end of every iteration, and it is process centric.

C· the agile team identifies the ways to improve its performance through a retrospective

D· Scrum master is the facilitator in the retrospective meeting

78. TechSoft Corporation is the leading Information Technology Company located in India. Shirley is the Scrum master working for the company for the last few years. Shirley had a discussion in one of the meetings about the purpose of the retrospective meeting. Identify the invalid purpose of the retrospective meeting from the given options?

A· the agile team identifies the ways to improve its performance through a retrospective

A· the agile team identifies the ways to improve its performance through a retrospective

C· an Agile retrospective is a meeting that's held at the end of an iteration and identify the areas that need improvement

D· the retrospective meeting used to happen at the end of every iteration, and it is process-centric.

79. Records of project inputs and outputs are called artifacts. Valid scrum artifacts are Product backlog, Sprint backlog, Product increment. Identify the valid Scrum artifacts from the given options?

A. Product backlog

B. Sprint backlog

C. Product increment

D. All of the above

80. Print Fast Corporation is a leading printing company located in Australia. Douglas is the Scrum master working for the company for the last few years. Douglas had a discussion in one of the meetings about the purpose of the scrum artifacts. Identify the purpose of the scrum artifacts from the given options?

A· Scrum Artifacts provides information that the Scrum Team and the stakeholders need to be aware of the product under development

B· Scrum Artifacts provides information that the Scrum Team and the stakeholders need to be aware of the product activities being planned

C. Both Option A and B are correct

D. Option A is correct

81. Quality Metals Corporation is a leading metals company located in London. Heather is the Scrum master working for the company for the last few years. Heather had a discussion in one of the

meetings about the scrum artifacts. Identify the valid scrum artifacts from the given options?

A. Product backlog

B. Sprint backlog,

C. Product increment

D. All of the above

82. Tech device Corporation is a leading Analog devices company located in Brazil. Sean is the Scrum master working for the company for the last few years. Sean had a discussion in one of the meetings about the Characteristics of the product backlog. Identify the Characteristics of product backlog from the given options?

A· Good product backlog should exhibit the characteristics DEEP (Detailed, Emergent, estimable, prioritized)

B· Product backlog contains the set of features, fixes, bugs or any other activities that a development team will deliver in the upcoming

C. Both Option A and B are correct

D. Only Option A is correct

83. Trade Online Corporation is a leading online trading company located in Mexico. Megan is the Scrum master working for the company for the last few years. Megan had a discussion in one of the meetings about the purpose of the product backlog. Identify the purpose of product backlog from the given options?

A· It contains user stories. Top of the product backlog contains user stories with high priority.

B· Product backlog contains the set of features, fixes, bugs or any other activities that a development team will deliver in the upcoming iterations

C· Product backlog items can be updated by the product owner at any time, so it needs to maintained continuously

D. All of the above

84. Econo Travel Corporation is a leading travel agency located in Canada. Jacob is the Scrum master working for the company for the last few years. Jacob had a discussion in one of the meetings about the purpose of the sprint backlog. Identify the invalid option related to the purpose of the sprint backlog from the given options?

A· Sprint backlog contains high priority user stories from the product backlog.

B· Sprint backlog only can be updated by the scrum development team and it can decide new items can be added to the sprint backlog or items removed from the backlog

C· Scrum Master owns the sprint backlog

D· The Sprint Backlog contains a list of tasks in the form of user stories selected from the Product Backlog based upon the priority set by the Product Owner during Sprint Planning meeting

85. Trade Anytime Corporation is a leading online brokerage company located in South America. Katherine is the Scrum master working for the company for the last few years. Katherine had a discussion in one of the meetings about the Characteristics of the sprint backlog. Identify the invalid option related to the Characteristics of the sprint backlog from the given options?

A· Sprint backlog contains high priority user stories from the product backlog.

B· It contains the tasks that can be completed during the current project

C· The Sprint Backlog contains a list of tasks in the form of user stories selected from the Product Backlog based upon the priority set by the Product Owner during Sprint Planning meeting

D· Sprint backlog items are usually in the form of user stories

86. RR Retail Corporation is a leading Retail company located in France. Juan is the Scrum master working for the company for the last few years. Juan had a discussion in one of the meetings about the Importance of transparency of artifacts. Identify the Importance of transparency of artifacts from the given options?

A. If artifacts are not transparent, then they cannot be successfully inspected and risks may increase, costs may increase and decisions can be made incorrectly.

B. Transparency is important to the Scrum process, as it allows everyone to understand what is really happening in each sprint,

C. If artifacts are not transparent, then they cannot be successfully inspected and risks may increase, costs may increase and decisions can be made incorrectly.

D. All of the above

87. Perfect Construction is a leading Construction company located in Italy. Natalie is the Scrum master working for the company for the last few years. Natalie had a discussion in one of the meetings about the XP Framework. The XP framework emphasizes the practice of collective ownership, continuous

integration, and pair programming. Identify the Core principles of XP from the given options?

A. Pair programming

B. Refactoring

C. Collective code ownership

D. All of the above

88. **In TDD (Test Driven Development) first, the developer writes a (failing) test case that defines the desired improvement, then produces the minimum amount of code to pass that test, and finally refactor the new code. Identify the steps available in TDD?**

A. write a test

B. verify and validate the test

C. write product code & apply the test

D. All of the above

89. Health first is a leading healthcare provider company located in the Netherlands. Russell is the Scrum master working for the company for the last few years. Russell had a discussion in one of the meetings about the Lean. Lean focus on value stream mapping. Eliminate waste is the core principle of lean. Identify the Lean Principles from the given options?

A. eliminate waste

B. empower the team

C. deliver fast

D. All of the above

90. Kanban means Signal. The team should update the Kanban board as the work progresses on the project. Kanban is a process designed to help teams work together more effectively. Identify the Kanban principles from the given options?

A. Visualize the workflow

B. Limit the amount of work in progress

C. Enhance the workflow

D. All of the above

91. Feature Driven Development is an iterative software development methodology intended for use by large teams working on a project using object-oriented technology. Identify the steps available in Feature-driven development from the given options?

A.develop an overall model

B. build a feature list

C. plan by feature

D. All of the above

92. The current iteration ends, and the product owner/customer says the product didn't meet the acceptance criteria. Identify the response from the scrum master response from the given options?

A. Add it in the next iteration backlog.

B. Add it to the current iteration and extend the iteration duration

C. Add it to the bottom of the product backlog

D. Ignore the request from the customer/product owner

93. An information radiator is a Visual display of current work status, so interested persons can get the information without disturbing the team. Identify the Contents of Information Radiator from the given options?

A. Visual display of current work status

B. release plan

C. backlog

D. working agreements

94. Airspace unlimited is a leading Aerospace company located in Spain. Gloria is the Scrum master working for the company for the last few years. Gloria had a discussion in one of the meetings about the Collocated and distributed team. Identify the Collocated and distributed team's key factors to consider from the given options?

A. synchronizing communication

B. high communication bandwidth

C. Both Option A and B are correct

D. Only Option A is correct

95. Econo Financial Corporation is a leading financial company located in London. Bruce is the Scrum master working for the company for the last few years. Bruce had a discussion in one of the meetings about the XP roles. Identify the valid XP roles from the given options?

A. XP coach,

B. XP Customer

C. XP Programmer

D. All of the above

96. Affordable Sporting goods Corporation is a leading sports goods company located in Australia. Sarah is the Scrum master working for the company for the last few years. Sarah had a discussion in one of the meetings about the agile principles. Identify the invalid agile principles from the given options?

A. Welcome changing requirements, even late in development. Agile process harness change for the customer's competitive advantage.

B. Customer collaboration over contract negotiation

C. Deliver working software frequently from a couple of weeks to a couple of months with a preference to the shorter time scale.

D. Our highest priority is to satisfy the customer through early and continuous delivery of valuable software

97. Finance anytime is a leading sports goods company located in South America region. Catherine is the Scrum master working for the company for the last few years. Catherine had a discussion in one of the meetings about continuous integration. Identify the invalid option related to continuous integration from the given options?

A. All changes need to be approved by the change control manager before production deployment.

B. All code changes are checked in and tested every day.

C. Options A and B are correct

D. Only Option B is correct

98. Cosmetics For you is a leading Cosmetics company located in the Europe region. Michael is the Scrum master working for the company for the last few years. Michael had a discussion in one of the meetings about limiting the Work In progress principle. Identify the Limiting the Work In progress principle is associated?

A. Kaizen

B. Kanban

C. Fishbone diagram

D. Lean

99. Fly High Airlines is a leading airline company located in India. Jessica is the Scrum master working for the company for the last few years. Jessica had a discussion in one of the meetings about the roles of the Scrum team. Who is the single voice of the customer in SCRUM projects?

A. The project manager

B. the Product owner

C. The Sponsor

D. The Scrum Master

100. Insure for you is a leading Insurance company located in India. Linda is the Scrum master working for the company for the last few years. Linda had a discussion in one of the meetings about the primary and secondary value in the agile manifesto. Which value is the secondary value of the agile manifesto?

A. Contract negotiation

B. Working software

C. Customer collaboration

D. Responding to change

CSM PRACTICE EXAM 5: ANSWERS

1. Answer: Option C

- The purpose of being transparent in the scrum project is, it will create trust and bring the stakeholders together.
- Also being transparent it is easy to communicate and provide feedback in both

the directions without any hesitation in the scrum ceremonies.

2. Answer: Option D is correct

Some of the Scrum development team responsibilities are,

- Execute the sprint as per the plan and test the product backlog items
- Deliver the potentially releasable increment of "done" at the end of every sprint
- Help product owner/scrum master to prioritize user stories in product backlog during the sprint planning meeting
- Development team is a self-organizing cross-functional team

3. Answer: Option C

Product Owner responsibilities during sprint planning meetings are,

- Product owner explains the product backlog items to the scrum development team during the sprint planning meeting.
- Product owner explains the team the highest priority items in the backlog in the sprint planning meeting.
- Product owner is responsible to define user stories and prioritize the backlog items.

- Product owner answers all the questions related to the product to the team during the meeting.
- Development team clarifies all the doubts related to the requirement of the product in the product backlog so that high-level user story in the product backlog can be converted into tasks in the sprint backlog

4. Answer: Option C

Scrum Master Role during the Sprint Planning Meeting is

- Scrum master facilitates the sprint planning meeting.
- Scrum Master makes sure agreements are reached in the sprint goal and the agreed product backlog items are included in the sprint backlog.

5. Answer: Option D is correct.

Some of the Development team responsibilities in daily scrum meetings,

- The scrum development team participates in the daily standup meeting.
- Development team talks about the progress toward the spring goal, and any obstacles are in their way to reach the goal.

- Scrum development team reviews the common sprint goal and its progress in the meeting.

6. Answer: Option C is correct.

Some of the Product owner responsibilities in daily scrum meeting are,

- Product owner can join the meeting and listen and observe, but won't interact
- Product owner has no active role in the meeting.

7. Answer: Option C is correct.

Scrum master role in daily scrum

- Scrum master keeps the daily scrum within the specified 15-minute duration.
- Daily scrum meeting is mainly conducted for the development team. Others can participate in the meeting. Scrum Master ensures that other participants are not interrupting the meeting
- Scrum master make sure that daily scrum meeting happens same time same place.

8. Answer: Option D is correct.

Development team role in the sprint review meeting

- During sprint review the actual increment is reviewed.

- Development team reviews what went well in the sprint, and what impediments they faced during the sprint, and how they resolve the impediments.
- The product increment is validated against the spring goal that was planned in the sprint planning meeting.
- Main participants are a scrum development team, product owner, and scrum master.

9. Answer: Option C

Product owner role in the sprint review meeting,

- Product owner conducts the sprint review meeting and compares the product increments with the sprint goal that was planned in the sprint planning meeting.
- Development team gave a demo about the product that is developed in the sprint.
- Product owner and other stakeholders review the product increment and compares against what was planned and what was accomplished during the sprint.
- Key Participants are a scrum development team, product owner, and scrum master.
- 4 hour meeting in general for one month sprint.

10. Answer: Option C is correct.

Scrum master role in the sprint review

- Scrum master arranges the sprint review meeting immediately after the sprint.
- It is held at the end of the sprint. Development team, scrum master and product owner review the product increment.
- Development team gave a demo about the product that is developed in the sprint and explains what is done and what is not.
- Scrum master enforces the timeframe for the meeting.

11. Answer: Option C is correct.

Scrum master role in retrospective:

- Scrum master is the facilitator in the retrospective meeting.
- Issues are discussed in the retrospective, and scrum master makes sure it is addressed by the development team before the next sprint.
- Retrospective is mainly conducted for the scrum team to inspect and make improvements to their process.
- This meeting must be conducted after the sprint review but before the next sprint planning meeting.

12. Answer: Option C is correct.

Product owner role in retrospective

- Product owner participates in the retrospective to increase collaboration between them and the development team.
- Retrospectives are mainly for the scrum development team. Scrum master and product owner can participate in the meeting.
- Issues in the process are discussed in the retrospective, and scrum master makes sure it is addressed by the development team before the next sprint.

13. Answer: Option C is correct.

Why the Sprint Goal does not change during a Sprint

- Sprint goal describes the business purpose and value of the sprint and provides guidance to the development team.
- Sprint goal is the mutual commitment between the scrum development team and the product owner.
- Development team commits to meet the goal at the end of the sprint, and the product owner commits not to change the sprint goal during the sprint.
- Development team can update the sprint backlog items during the sprint.

14. **Answer: Option D is correct.**

The outcome of every Sprint:

- Every sprint must have one goal.
- The goal is defined before the start of the sprint.
- Sprint goal is achieved through the implementation of product backlog items.

15. Answer: Option D is correct.

Activities of the product owner during sprint planning

- Product owner represents the customer during the sprint planning meeting.
- Product owner and the development team jointly develop the objective of the upcoming sprint.
- During the sprint planning meeting Product owner explains the features developed during the next sprint and the development team clarifies all the doubts from the product owner.
- Sprint goal is developed/agreed during the sprint planning meeting.
- Development team decomposes the high-level user story defined by the product owner in the product backlog into detailed tasks for the sprint backlog.

16. Answer: Option D is correct.

Activities of the development team during sprint planning:

- In the spring planning meeting, the scrum development team establishes the goals for the next sprint along with the product owner and scrum master.
- During the first session the Product Owner presents the highest priorities of the Product Backlog to the team.
- The highest priority items from the backlog, the development team agrees to develop for the upcoming next sprint.
- Development team decomposes the high-level user story defined by the product owner in the product backlog into detailed tasks for the sprint backlog.
- Development team agrees to complete a set of product backlog items.

17. Answer: Option D is correct.

How to write a sprint goal

- Sprint goals should be SMART (specific, measurable, attainable, relevant and time-bounded)
- It is achieved by implementing the product backlog items.
- In general goal is written as 1 to 2 sentences and describes what is going to be developed by the scrum development team in the upcoming sprint.

- It is developed by negotiation between the development team and product owner and it is developed collaboratively.

18. Answer: Option C is correct.

Daily scrum differs from a status meeting

- Daily scrum meeting is not a status meeting to update project status.
- This meeting is conducted for the development team to synchronize the development of team activities.
- It helps the development team to self-organize and empowered to make their own decisions.
- Daily scrum meeting is time-boxed to 15 minutes and it happens daily at the same time and at the same place.
- 3 questions are asked in the daily scrum meeting. What did they do yesterday, and what the development team is planning to do today, and if there are any obstacles on their way.
- Daily scrum meeting improves team collaboration.

19. Answer: Option D is correct.

Activities that occur during the Sprint Review

- Sprint review meeting is attended by the scrum development team, product owner, and the scrum master.
- Development team discusses the increment they developed during the sprint and further they explain what went well, what the impediments they faced are, and how they resolve the issues.
- Product increment is assessed against what was originally planned in the sprint planning meeting.
- Product owner discusses the work done in the product backlog and the work not done from the product backlog.
- Scrum development team justifies the increment that they developed during the sprint.
- Sprint review meeting provides feedback for the next sprint planning meeting.

20. Answer: Option C is correct.

Potential outcomes for a Sprint Review:

- Development team presents the increment that they developed during the sprint review.
- One of the outcomes of the sprint review meeting is revised product backlog items, which is going to be developed in the next sprint.
- The product backlog is adjusted against the new risks and opportunities.

21. Answer: Option D is correct

Approaches to conducting a Sprint Retrospective

- Sprint retrospective occurs after the sprint review but before the next sprint planning.
- In the meeting discuss what went well during the sprint, and what went not well and how to improve the process

22. Answer: Option D is correct

Attributes of a Product Backlog item

- Some of the attributes are product description, order, value, the definition of done, work to be completed, and estimation
- Product backlogs contain user stories related to requirements, defects, etc.

23. **Answer: Option C is correct.**

Essential characteristics of the Sprint Backlog

- Sprint backlog contains high priority user stories from the product backlog.
- Development team decomposes the high-level user story defined by the product owner in the product backlog into detailed tasks for the current iteration.

- Exhibits the characteristics DEEP (detailed, estimable, emergent and prioritized)

24. Answer: Option C

How the Sprint Backlog can be changed without endangering the Sprint Goal

- Sprint goal should not be changed during the sprint.
- If we change the Sprint goal changes it results in alteration of work, change of scope, waste
- Sprint backlog only can be updated by the scrum development team. They update the backlog with completed work and the remaining work. If needed eliminate added work in the backlog and add the new work to the backlog. This can be only done by the development team.
- Only the development team can change the items in the sprint backlog.

25. Answer: Option D is correct.

Importance of a strong definition of done scrum

- The scrum development team can have its own definition of done.
- If the definition of done is done correctly it will avoid rework, waste.
- One of the advantages of the definition of done is correctly, then the chances of acceptance of

the product by the product owner/customer is more.

- By using the definition of done, we can assess the quality of the work done for the product or product increment.
- Once the user story is completed by the development team, we can assess the quality of work by using the definition of done.
- By having a strong definition of done, prevent the lower quality products or product increments handed over to the customer.

26. Answer: Option D is correct.

Risks associated with a weaker definition of done scrum

- The definition of done should be defined correctly. Weaker definition of done results in customer dissatisfaction, risks, and delays.
- Weaker definition of done results in chances of acceptance of the product by the product owner/customer is less.
- Weaker definition of done results in partial product working, and part of increment is not working.
- It develops a false sense of progress about the product developed in the sprint.

27. **Answer: Option D is correct.**

- The definition of done is created by the scrum development team.
- Acceptance criteria in the definition of done are created by the product owner.
- When the product increment met the acceptance criteria the will be accepted by the customer/product owner.

28. Answer: Option C is correct.

Reasons why multiple teams working on the same Product Backlog have a shared and consistent definition of "Done."

- If the project is very big in size, sometimes it is executed by multiple scrum development teams. If multiple teams are working on the product, then all the teams mutually define the definition of done for the product.
- Even though it is mutually defined by all the scrum teams, every team maintains its own product backlog.

29. Answer: Option D is correct.

Scrum Master Core Competencies

- They facilitate meetings daily scrum meetings, sprint planning meetings, sprint review, and sprint retrospective.
- Shield the team from interruptions
- Remove impediments
- Conflict resolution
- Coaching the team with agile practices

30. Answer: Option C is correct

How Scrum Master helps the scrum team by facilitation

- Scrum master helps the scrum team by facilitating scrum events like sprint planning, daily scrum meeting, and scrum review and sprint retrospectives.
- Scrum master facilitates the development team in delivering the product increment by ensuring the team follows the Scrum practices.

31. Answer: Option D is correct.

Scrum techniques for facilitating group decision making

The three types of group decision making are the nominal group technique, Delphi technique, and brainstorming.

32 Answer: Option B is correct.

Nominal group technique:

It is derived from a brainstorming technique. It involves a voting process to rank the ideas generated. The ideas which have more votes will be selected as the result of the session. In this technique, ideas are generated using brainstorming in a small group environment and then reviewed by a larger group.

33. Answer: Option A is correct.

Delphi technique: This technique is used to get the opinions of experts. In this technique, instead of everybody in the same room, the questionnaire is sent to risk experts and asking about the risks in the project. Once the questionnaire is collected, it was recirculated again to reach the consensus in opinion. It will take a few rounds to reach the consensus. In this technique, nobody knows about who else is involved in this process.

34. Answer: Option C is correct.

Brainstorming is a group creativity technique by which efforts are made to find a conclusion for a specific problem by gathering a list of ideas spontaneously contributed by its members.

35. Answer: Option D is correct.

Difference between coaching and facilitation:

- Coaching is more directive in nature than the facilitation
- Facilitation helps the groups as well as the individual teams
- Both coaching and facilitation helps the team to improve the performance

36. Answer: Option D is correct.

- Scrum Master as Servant-Leader
- Shield the team from interruptions
- Coach the team regarding the self-organization
- Coaching the team in adopting scrum in the organization
- Encourage collaboration between the members of the scrum team
- Focus on the needs of the team members with the goal of achieving results aligned with organizational goals.
- Encourage the team for healthy debates
- Encourage the scrum team to reach their potential

37. Answer: Option C is correct.

- Remove impediments for the scrum team

- Coaching the team in adopting scrum in the organization
- Coach the team regarding the self-organization, and not telling them what to do
- Focus on the needs of the team members with the goal of achieving results aligned with organizational goals
- Helps the team to take responsibility for their actions
- Coach the team with the problem-solving techniques

38. Answer: Option C is correct.

- Scrum development teamwork may be disturbed by the product owner or other key stakeholders in the project. Scrum Master makes sure it won't happen in their project.
- Some of the user stories in the product backlog are kept without the proper acceptance criteria.
- Last minute changes can be introduced by the product owner in the sprint. This needs to be avoided. Scrum master needs to deal with this scenario.
- Product backlog contains items more than the development team's capacity. This also needs to be avoided.
- User stories in the backlog have enough details and it should be estimable.

- The product owner or stakeholders can distract the daily scrum meeting. The scrum master must step in and avoid the distractions.

39. Answer: Option C is correct

- The tasks related to technical debt must be entered into the product backlog so that the scrum team is aware of that.
- Always allocate some percentage of tasks to deal with the defect fixing.
- Bring up the topic related to technical debt in the sprint review meeting, so that everyone aware of that and discuss dealing it.

40. Answer: Option C is correct.

- Work closely with the product owner and keep the product backlog updated for the upcoming sprints.
- Scrum master helps the product owner and the scrum development team to follow the correct processes and agile principles and help them to choose the correct tools & techniques.

41. Answer: Option C is correct

- Product owner participates in the retrospective to increase collaboration between them and the development team.

- Retrospectives are mainly for the scrum development team. Scrum master and product owner can participate in the meeting.

42. Answer: Option C is correct.

- Remove impediments for the scrum team. Sometimes scrum team will remove the impediments on their own. In case if they are not able to remove the impediments then the scrum master helps to remove it.
- Scrum master adds the impediments in the product backlog and works with the development team to remove the impediments.

43. Answer: Option D is correct.

3 organizational impediments that can affect Scrum Teams.

- Organizational culture
- Lack of training or knowledge by the team
- Over commitment for the sprint or release.
- Organizational and technical impediments

44. Answer: Option C is correct.

Example of an organizational design change caused by adopting Scrum

Some of the changes caused by adopting scrum are,

- Teams can be cross-functional
- Departments can be merged into a single department based on the product group.
- Total number of managers may be decreased

45. Answer: Option C is correct.

- Scrum only defines 3 roles Scrum Master, Product Owner, and development team
- Project manager is outside of the scrum team, and there is no role as project manager defined in scrum projects
- Project manager is responsible for the project

46. Answer: Option C is correct

Definition of Scrum:

- Scrum is a framework for agile software development.
- Scrum projects progress through a series of iterations called sprints.
- Each sprint is 2-4 weeks long.
- Scrum is suited for projects with changing requirements.
- Scrum teams commit to shipping working software through sprints

47. Answer: Option C is correct

Relationship of Scrum to Agile:

- Agile describes a set of guiding principles that uses an iterative approach for software development
- Scrum is a specific set of rules that are to be followed while practicing the agile software development
- Agile is a continuous iteration of development and testing in the software development process whereas Scrum is an agile process to focus on delivering the business value in the shortest time

48. Answer: Option C is correct

Empirical process control as it relates to scrum

- In Scrum, an empirical process is implemented where progress is based on observation and experimentation instead of detailed, upfront planning and defined processes.
- Empirical process relies on the three main ideas of transparency, inspection, and adaptation

49. Answer: Option C is correct.

How and why “incremental” is an important characteristic of scrum:

- Scrum is incremental because work is delivered throughout the project at regular intervals through iterations

- Instead of getting the feedback at the end of the final product, the feedback is obtained for every increment. This helps the team to make changes early and often.

50. Answer: Option D is correct.

Applicability of Scrum

- Scrum is an agile process most commonly used for software development
- Scrum is also applicable to any projects with tight timelines, complex requirements, and requirements are not known at the beginning of the project
- Scrum increase team collaboration and increase improve communication between the team members

51. Answer: Option D is correct.

5 core scrum values are Commitment, Focus, Openness, Respect, and Courage

52. Answer: Option C is correct.

Commitment is an important scrum value.

- Scrum teams agree to complete tasks that they believe they can complete, so they won't overcommit.
- Development team commits in the scrum project by creating an increment according to the definition of done
- Scrum master shows commitment to the project by not extending the duration of the sprint, also commit to removing the impediments that can't be handled by the development team
- Product backlog shows commitment to transparency
- Retrospective proves the commitment for continuous improvement

53. Answer: Option D is correct

How and why courage is an important Scrum value

- Scrum team have the courage to do the right thing
- Team has the courage to ask for help and to take calculated risks in the project
- Scrum master have the courage to remove impediments that blocks the team's progress and also stop the last minute's changes introduced in the sprint

54. Answer: Option D is correct.

How and why focus is an important Scrum value

- Scrum master allows the team to focus and define their own definition of done
- Scrum team focus on only the work to be done in a sprint by limiting the work in progress that eliminates waste
- Scrum team focus on delivering the increment as per the definition of done at the end of every sprint

55. Answer: Option D is correct.

- Openness allows the scrum team to share their opinions openly and heard by the teams.
- Openness allows the team to allow the team if they are done anything wrong and able the team to correct from their mistakes
- Openness supports transparency

56. Answer: Option B is not related to self-organizing. It is related to a cross-functional team.

- Self-organizing is an important characteristic of Scrum teams
- In scrum self-organization promotes shared ownership.
- Increase the chances of team buy-in
- Self-organization promotes innovative ideas in the project
- Increase in efficiency
- Increase the motivation of the scrum team

57. Answer: Option B is not correct. It is one of the characteristics of self-organizing teams.

Cross-functional is an essential characteristic of Scrum teams

- Cross-functional makes the scrum team successful
- Cross-functional team has all skills necessary to accomplish the product without depending on other teams that are not part of the scrum team.
- It increases the creativity and problem-solving skills of the team members.
- The members of the team has diverse experience, skills which are essential to complete the project successfully

58. Answer: Option C is not correct. There is no role as a project manager in Scrum projects.

3 Roles in Scrum: Product Owner, Development Team, Scrum master

59. Answer: Option B is not correct. It is one of the main responsibilities of the product owner.

Responsibilities of the Scrum Master

- Teaching Scrum and seeing that it is adopted and used correctly.
- Remove impediments for the scrum team

- Protect the team from distractions
- Establish the environment that the scrum team can work effectively
- Coach/mentor to the scrum team

60. Answer: Option C is not correct. It is related to the characteristics of the product owner.

Characteristics of a scrum master

- Coach agile practices to the team
- Remove impediments for the team
- Create the environment that communication is smooth between the scrum team and product owner
- Protects the team from distractions
- Facilitate scrum ceremonies

61. Answer: Option B is not correct. It is one of the main responsibilities of the product owner.

Scrum product owner responsibilities

- The product owner is responsible for product vision and responsible for prioritizing and reprioritizing product backlog.
- They answer questions related to the product requirements to the development team. They can decide whether to accept or reject the project.
- Prioritize the items in the product backlog

- Responsible to define the user stories in the product backlog

62. Answer: Option C is not correct. It is related to the characteristics of the Scrum master.

Characteristics of a product owner

- They must have good domain knowledge and good communication skills
- They should be available when needed by the development team
- Clear communication with the development team and understand their concerns and guide them towards the product vision
- Responsible to define and prioritize user stories in the product backlog
- Convey the needs of the stakeholders to the development team to develop the right product

63. Answer: Option C is not correct. It is one of the responsibilities of the scrum master.

Scrum development team responsibilities

- Develop the product backlog items into increments of potentially shippable functionality as agreed during the sprint
- Develop the product as per the definition of done

- Work with the product owner and scrum master in the sprint planning meeting to prioritize the product backlog items
- Cross-functional team responsible for the product

64. Answer: Option B is not correct. It is one of the characteristics of the Product owner.

Characteristics of the scrum development team

- They are self-organizing
- Development team is cross-functional
- No sub-teams in the development team, the team members have all the necessary skills to develop the product

65. Answer: Option B is invalid. It is the responsibility of the product owner.

Scrum Master -- servant-leader for the Scrum team

- They are servant leaders for the scrum team, manages the team not by telling them what to do
- They coach the team to follow agile/Scrum principles
- Remove impediments
- Focus on the needs of the team members with the goal of achieving results aligned with organizational goals.

66. Answer: Option C is not correct. It is one of the responsibilities of the Scrum development team.

Scrum Master Service to the Organization

- Coach the scrum team and organization to follow scrum practices
- Create changes and increase the productivity of the development team
- Coach, the team, to self-organize
- Help the team to create product increment and remove the impediments for the team
- Work with the product owner related to the product backlog and make sure it is ready for the next sprint

67. Answer: Option C is not correct. It is the characteristics of product backlog.

Characteristics of the sprint:

- At the beginning of the sprint, the goals are defined.
- Scrum team works towards the goal during the sprint
- At the end of the sprint entire team with the product owner review the developed product during the sprint, and if variations are found then the adjustments are made.

68. Answer: Option A is not correct. · Every sprint starts with a sprint planning meeting and ends with a sprint review.

Purpose of sprint

- Sprint is a time-boxed iteration and the agreed work is completed during the sprint
- Deliver the increment of the product as per the definition of done is the main purpose of the sprint
- Every sprint starts with a sprint planning meeting and ends with a sprint review
- Scrum development team delivers the increment of functionality at every sprint

69. Answer: Option C is not correct. Result of the sprint planning meeting is sprint backlog and sprint goal that the team agreed

Characteristics of sprint planning in scrum:

- Every sprint has a sprint planning meeting which happens at the beginning of the sprint
- The Scrum development team agreed to develop the increment of the product during that sprint
- Sprint planning meeting is attended by the scrum development team, product owner and the scrum master
- During the meeting product owner explains the highest priority items in the backlog

- Development team agreed to complete the items as per the agreement in the meeting
- It is time-boxed meeting
- The development team is in agreement with the product owner that they develop the specific features as defined in the backlog
- Result of the sprint planning meeting is sprint backlog and sprint goal that the team agreed

70. Answer: Option B is not correct. It is one of the roles of the Product Owner.

Participant's role in the sprint planning meeting

- Product owner explains the backlog and defines the highest priority items in the backlog. Also, they define the sprint goal along with the sprint development team
- Scrum master facilitates the sprint planning meeting
- Development team defines the sprint goal along with the product owner and pick the sprint backlog items from the product backlog

71. Answer: Option C is correct.

Purpose of the Sprint planning meeting:

- Define the increment that is going to be delivered in the upcoming sprint, and how the team is going to deliver

- Development team determines the product backlog items they will deliver during the sprint

72. Answer: Option B is not correct. It is conducted mostly for the development team to synchronize their activities and improve the communication between the development team

Characteristics of daily standup meeting in scrum

- Daily standup meeting is time-boxed and it happens at the same place and at the same time
- It is the short meeting has a duration of 15 minutes
- It is conducted mostly for the development team to synchronize their activities and improve the communication between the development team
- They discuss the user stories developed and the impediments for their work

73. Answer: Option C is correct.

Value of daily standup meeting in scrum

- This is conducted for the development team and the team discuss the user stories that they developed, not developed and if there are any impediments on their way
- It helps the communication between the team members, and identify the impediments that stop their work

74. Answer: Option B is invalid. There is no project manager role in Scrum projects.

Role of participants in daily standup meeting in scrum

- All the development team members must attend the daily standup meeting
- Scrum master and product owner also attend the meeting
- This is conducted for the development team and the team discuss the user stories that they developed, not developed and if there are any impediments on their way
- Scrum Master Coaches the team to keep the daily standup meeting within 15 minutes duration
- If other stakeholders participate, they should not interrupt the meeting.

75. Answer: Option B is not correct. The sprint review meeting is held at the end of the sprint.

Characteristics of a sprint review meeting

- Development team explains about the product and discuss what went well and what not went well during the sprint and the obstacles they faced
- It is held at the end of the sprint
- It is conducted to inspect the product features developed during the sprint

76. Answer: Option B is not correct. · The development team gave a demo about the product that is developed in the sprint.

Role of participants in the sprint review meeting:

- Product owner conducts the sprint review meeting and compares the product increments with the sprint goal that was planned in the sprint planning meeting.
- Development team gave a demo about the product that is developed in the sprint.
- Product owner and other stakeholders review the product increment and compares against what was planned and what was accomplished during the sprint.
- Scrum master arranges the sprint review meeting immediately after the sprint.

77. Answer: Option A is not correct. It is one of the Characteristics of the sprint review meeting.

Characteristics of the retrospective meeting

- Scrum master is the facilitator in the retrospective meeting
- The retrospective meeting used to happen at the end of every iteration, and it is process centric.
- The agile team identifies the ways to improve its performance through a retrospective

- In this meeting, the team identifies the ways to improve deliverables
- The attendees of retrospective meeting are the development team, scrum master and product owner

78. Answer: Option B is not correct. · The retrospective meeting used to happen at the end of every iteration, and it is process centric.

Purpose of the retrospective meeting

- The retrospective meeting used to happen at the end of every iteration, and it is process centric.
- The agile team identifies the ways to improve its performance through a retrospective
- An Agile retrospective is a meeting that's held at the end of an iteration and identify the areas that need improvement
- Create a plan to implement the improvement

79. Answer: Option D is correct.

Scrum artifacts

- Valid scrum artifacts are Product backlog, Sprint backlog, Product increment
- Records of project inputs and outputs are called artifacts
- 2 Main Artifacts of sprint planning meeting are sprint goal and sprint backlog

80. Answer: Option C is correct.

Purpose of Scrum artifacts

- Scrum Artifacts provides information that the Scrum Team and the stakeholders need to be aware of the product under development, the activities being planned, and the activities are done in the project.

81. Answer: Option D is correct.

Valid scrum artifacts are Product backlog, Sprint backlog, Product increment

82. Answer: Option C is correct.

Characteristics of product backlog:

- Good product backlog should exhibit the characteristics DEEP (Detailed, Emergent, estimable, prioritized)
- Product backlog contains the set of features, fixes, bugs or any other activities that a development team will deliver in the upcoming iterations
- It contains user stories. Top of the product backlog contains user stories with the high priority

83. Answer: Option D is correct.

Purpose of product backlog:

- It contains user stories. Top of the product backlog contains user stories with high priority.
- Risks, costs are some of the factors considered for prioritizing the product backlog
- Product backlog contains the set of features, fixes, bugs or any other activities that a development team will deliver in the upcoming iterations
- Product owner along with the scrum development team prioritize the backlog
- Product backlog items can be updated by the product owner at any time, so it needs to maintained continuously

84. Answer: Option C is not correct. · Development team owns the sprint backlog

Purpose of the sprint backlog

- Sprint backlog contains high priority user stories from the product backlog.
- Development team decomposes the high-level user story defined by the product owner in the product backlog into detailed tasks for the current iteration.
- Exhibits the characteristics DEEP (detailed, estimable, emergent and prioritized)

- Sprint backlog only can be updated by the scrum development team and it can decide new items can be added to the sprint backlog or items removed from the backlog
- Development team owns the sprint backlog
- Sprint backlog contains tasks identified by the development team that need to be completed in the sprint
- The Sprint Backlog contains a list of tasks in the form of user stories selected from the Product Backlog based upon the priority set by the Product Owner during Sprint Planning meeting
- If the development team is unable to complete the user stories in the sprint backlog by the end of the sprint, the team can add those unfinished user stories to the next sprint backlog

85. Answer: Option B is not correct. It contains the tasks that can be completed during the current sprint

Characteristics of a sprint backlog

- Sprint backlog contains high priority user stories from the product backlog.
- The Sprint Backlog contains a list of tasks in the form of user stories selected from the Product Backlog based upon the priority set by the Product Owner during Sprint Planning meeting
- It contains the tasks that can be completed during the current sprint

- Sprint backlog items are usually in the form of user stories
- Sprint backlog contains tasks identified by the development team that need to be completed in the sprint

86. Answer: Option D is correct.

Importance of transparency of artifacts

- If artifacts are not transparent, then they cannot be successfully inspected and risks may increase, costs may increase and decisions can be made incorrectly.
- The Scrum Master works with the Product Owner, Development Team, and other involved parties to make sure the artifacts are completely transparent
- Transparency is important to the Scrum process, as it allows everyone to understand what is really happening in each sprint,

87. Answer: Option D is correct.

XP

The framework emphasizes the practice of collective ownership, continuous integration, and pair programming.

Core principles of XP.

- Planning game
- Small releases
- Simple design
- product theme
- TDD (test-driven development)
- Refactoring
- Pair programming
- Collective code ownership
- Continuous integration.

88. Answer: Option D is correct.

TDD (Test Driven Development)

First, the developer writes a (failing) test case that defines the desired improvement, then produces the minimum amount of code to pass that test, and finally refactor the new code.

The steps are

- write a test
- verify and validate the test
- write product code & apply the test
- Refactor the product code.

89. Answer: Option D is correct.

Lean process

Lean focus on value stream mapping. Eliminate waste is the core principle of lean. Lean Principles

- Eliminate waste
- Empower the team
- Deliver fast
- Optimize the whole
- Build in quality
- Defer decisions
- Amplify learning.

90. Answer: Option D is correct.

Kanban

Kanban means Signal. The team should update the Kanban board as the work progresses on the project. Kanban is a process designed to help teams work together more effectively. It is based on 3 basic principles

- Visualize the workflow
- Limit the amount of work in progress
- Enhance the workflow

91. Answer: Option D is correct.

FDD (Feature-driven development)

Feature Driven Development is an iterative software development methodology intended for use by large teams working on a project using object-oriented technology.

- develop an overall model
- build a feature list
- plan by feature
- design by feature
- build by feature

92. Answer: Option A is correct.

Add it in the next iteration backlog.

93. Answer: Option D is correct.

Contents of Information Radiator

Visual display of current work status, so interested persons can get the information without disturbing the team. It has product vision, backlog, release plan, burn up, burn down chart, and working agreements.

94. Answer: Option C is correct.

Collocated and distributed team's key factors to consider are

- synchronizing communication
- high communication bandwidth

95. Answer: Option D is correct.

XP Roles are,

-XP coach, XP Customer, XP Programmer, XP Tracker, XP Tester.

96. Answer: Option B is not correct. It is related to the Agile Manifesto.

Agile Principles

1. Our highest priority is to satisfy the customer through early and continuous delivery of valuable software

2. Welcome changing requirements, even late in development. Agile process harness change for the customer's competitive advantage.

3. Deliver working software frequently from a couple of weeks to a couple of months with a preference to the shorter time scale.

97. Answer: Option D is correct.

Continuous-integration

All code changes are checked in and tested every day.

98. Answer: B

Explanation: Kanban is a process designed to help teams work together more effectively. It is based on 3 basic principles,

- Visualize the workflow
- Limit the work in progress
- Enhance the workflow

All other choices are not correct.

The Fishbone diagram is used to identify the root cause of the issue.

Kaizen is the Japanese management philosophy of continuous improvement.

Lean focus on value stream mapping. Eliminate waste is the core principle of lean.

99. Answer: B

Explanation: The product owner is the single point of contact for customers in SCRUM. They are the voice of customers and represent stakeholders and businesses, setting priorities, and deliverables. Other choices PM, sponsor, and scrum master are not correct.

100. Answer: A

Explanation: Agile manifesto (highlighted values on the right-hand side are secondary values).

- Individuals and interactions over **process and tools**.
- Working software over **comprehensive documentation**.
- Customer collaboration over **contract negotiation**.
- Responding to change over **following a plan.**

•

Flashcard Practice:

Story size specified by	Ideal days, actual days, story points.
Story points	Used to quantify the work effort and complexity required to develop a user story related to other stories.
Daily standup usage	-to synchronize team member's activities
Iteration Review meeting	- occurs at the end of an iteration - team present work product to stakeholders, so that they can review the product and give feedback.

Retrospective meeting	-Held at the end of every iteration -Process centric meeting
Management asked the agile team for a detailed project plan. The response of the agile coach is to	Take the opportunity to educate senior management on agile principles.
Coach sees an increase in the number of escaped defects, which are traced back to a developer. what action does he need to take	Address this issue with the team.
Purpose of an iteration retrospective	To improve future iterations.
The person that manages the iteration backlog	Team

When a team releases a build that is not in compliance with the organizational standard.	This contributes to technical debt.
Scrum of Scrum meetings	Multiple agile projects handled by multiple teams are co-coordinated
Sprint Ceremony	Sprint planning Daily standup, Sprint Retrospective.
User stories at the bottom of the backlog	Not well defined as the ones at the top of the backlog.
In agile project, schedule is built	By estimating story points and applying velocity.
Disagreement over the order in the iteration backlog is dealt by	The team.
The current iteration ends, and the customer says the product didn't	Add it in the next iteration backlog.

meet the acceptance criteria. As a scrum master, the response is	
Artifacts	Records of project inputs and outputs are called
Scrum Master	The person who ensures that process is followed and shields the team from interferences.
Roadmap	Highest level of time box composed of release plans.
Iteration handoff	Work to prepare formal documentation and other deliverables that are needed for the project.
Agile empirical process	Transparency, inspection, adoption.
Acceptance criteria	Written on the back of the story card.

Soft commitment:	The team makes a soft commitment to a specific set of features for the iteration backlog
Hard commitment:	Once the team finishes their analysis, they make a hard commitment to a specific set of features to be delivered at the end of the iteration to the product owner.
Collocated and distributed team's key factors to consider:	-synchronizing communication -high communication bandwidth
Time boxed Plan	When a project's due date is fixed due to regulations, it needs to be completed by a certain date.
Estimating technique used to determine the development effort	sizing

required to complete the user stories	
The department manager asked the scrum master to calculate the team labor cost for the coming iteration. They are looking for	Team's burn rate
Agile Team has some private space to make phone calls, personal work, etc.,	caves and commons
It is one of the risk mitigation technique used in an agile environment that developers need to continuously integrate their code to verify recent changes haven't broken the base code, which is already developed -	continuous integration
It means the product is coded, tested, defect-free, and accepted by the product owner.	Done Done

The iteration, the team stops focusing on delivering new features and instead spends its time on stabilizing the system and getting it ready to be release	Hardening iteration
The tool which represents the work remaining on the project is called	Product backlog
The meeting is for the team to show the customers and stakeholders the work they have done for the current iteration	Product Demo
The activity that a team review its performance for the purpose of improving its performance which is held at the end of every iteration	Retrospective meeting

Used to transfer a product from development to operations.	Hand off iteration
prototyping	One of the agile feedback technique for the product.
Product roadmap	Serves as a high level overview of product requirement.
Acceptance criteria	Written on the back of the story card.
Servant leadership skills	mentoring -guiding the team -create environment for personal safety

	-remove obstacles that stop progress -facilitating
Participatory decision making	Ownership of decision belongs to the team.
Time boxed plan	When a project's due date is fixed due to regulations, it needs to be completed by certain date.
Product Roadmap	Customer's vision at high level.
Iteration zero(planning iteration)	Used for foundation work, before the actual work begins for a project.
User stories	Description of product written from the perspective on end user, who is using the product.
Iteration backlog	Prioritized user stories in the product backlog that the team is committed to

	develop during a particular iteration.
Reciprocal commitment	Team commits to complete the user stories agreed in the iteration backlog, and the product owner is not changing the priorities during the iteration.
Sizing	Estimating technique used to determine development effort required to complete the user stories.
Story size specified by	Ideal days, actual days, story points.
Ideal days	Time required to complete an activity assuming there are no interruptions, so that work can be completed 100% efficiently.

Actual days	Time required to complete an activity that considers typical interruptions, that results in efficiency below 100%.
Story points	Used to quantify the work effort and complexity required to develop a user story related to other stories.
Burn up chart	Shows work completed in story points.
Kanban board	-tools used for continuous improvement. -by using this value stream map can be created.
Iteration Review meeting	-occurs at the end of iteration - team present work product to stakeholders, so that they can review

	the product and give feedback.
Retrospective meeting	-Held at the end of every iteration -Process centric meeting
Relative sizing	Placing stories on the wall in the order of the greatest to the least called.
Coach sees an increase in the number of escaped defects, which are traced back to a developer. what action does he need to take	Address this issue with the team.
Management asked the agile team for a detailed project plan. The response of the agile coach is to	Take the opportunity to educate the senior management on agile principles.
Purpose of iteration retrospective	To improve future iterations.

In agile, the time-frame to deliver the working software	From a couple of weeks to a couple of months.
The person that manages the iteration backlog	Team
When a team releases a build that is not in compliance with the organizational standard.	This contributes to technical debt.
Scrum of Scrum meetings	Multiple agile projects handled by multiple teams are co-coordinated
Sprint Ceremony	Sprint planning Daily standup, Sprint Retrospective.
User stories at the bottom of the backlog	Not well defined as the ones in the top of the backlog.
In agile project, schedule is built	By estimating story points and applying velocity.

Disagreement over the order in the iteration backlog is dealt by	The team.
The current iteration ends, and the customer says the product didn't meet the acceptance criteria. As a scrum master, the response is	Add it in the next iteration backlog.
Scrum Master	The person who ensures that process is followed and shields the team from interferences.
Roadmap	Highest level of time box composed of release plans.
Iteration handoff	Work to prepare formal documentation and other deliverables that are needed for the project.

Risk adjusted backlog	Defines feature priorities, taking into consideration of regulatory requirements.
73, role of product owner in daily scrum meeting	The product owner has no role in the daily Scrum meeting. The product owner can attend the daily scrum meeting. It is mainly for the Scrum team.
Product owner role	Clarify and convey the needs of stakeholders to the development team. Also, make sure the scrum development team gets the correct information to make the product in the iteration.
User story	The product owner, as well as the scrum team, can write user stories for the sprint.

Glossary

Acceptance criteria

Written on the back of the story card. It defines the limits of the user story. It helps the team to understand better what the user wants to accept a product developed by the development team.

Agile manifesto

- Individuals and interactions over process and tools.
- Working software over comprehensive documentation.
- Customer collaboration over contract negotiation.
- Responding to change over following a plan

Agile modeling

- It is a collection of values, principles, and practices used to create models for software development projects. Some core values of agile modeling are that it is simple, easy to communicate, getting feedback from the customer proxy/product owner, based on that team can confirm if they are on track with their development efforts.

Artifact

- Records of project inputs and outputs are called artifacts. E.g. of artifacts in the agile product backlog, product vision statement, product roadmap, etc.

Backlog grooming

- It is a process of reviewing, adding, deleting, and re-prioritizing user stories that are considered to be important to the customer. Generally, the agile team has a backlog grooming session once per iteration.

Burn-down chart

- It is a type of information radiator. It shows the work remaining in story points or ideal days in a project. A burndown chart is a graphical representation of work left for a given period. Burndown chart provides a way to track the progress of the project daily.

Burn rate

- It is the cost of an agile team or the rate at which it consumes resources.

Burn up chart

- It shows both planned work and completed work during an iteration. It tracks the progress of the project towards completion. It is used to identify instantly if there is any deviation from the planned project work. It is used to communicate to the project stakeholders how the additional requests they are asking for will affect the deadline of the project, and at the same time for reassuring them that good progress is being made in the project.

Collocation

- Ideal team member location in an agile environment. Ideally, the entire agile team will be located in the same place– not just the same office but sitting side by side in the same room or space. Having co-located teams improve communication, closer working relationships, collaboration, and enables face-to-face communication.

Continuous improvement

- Team retrospective is one type of continuous improvement. In Japanese kaizen is the word used for improvement. The retrospective is used for the process improvement in teamwork. Continuous improvement is a method for identifying opportunities for streamlining work and reducing waste.

Cross-functional team

- A cross-functional team is a team that combines specialists in different areas that are required to reach their set goals. Cross-functional means that the team as a whole has all skills needed to build the product, and that each team member is willing to do more than just their own thing.

Cycle time

- Time taken for the work from start to finish (value to be produced) is called cycle time.

Daily standup meeting

- It is conducted mainly to synchronize team member's activities. It happens always at the same time, the same location. Generally, it will be 15 minutes, and the time won't be extended for any reason. It is not the status update meeting for the management. It is used to identify the issues before they become problematic.

3 questions mainly asked in the daily meet up,

- What did we do yesterday?
- What are we planning to do today?
- Are there any obstacles blocking the way to do the task?

Dashboard

- It is a type of information radiator that uses red, green, and yellow colors to indicate the status of the project. It shows the day-to-day information that the team provides so that the management knows about the project.

Decomposition

- An agile team is dividing the user stories, into smaller, manageable tasks. The process is called decomposition. E.g. of decomposition.

- ❖ Epic- user story-task (Epic can be decomposed into user stories. User stories can be decomposed into tasks to do)

Done

- It is determined by the team. Both team and product owner decide what "done" means to the project. A list of criteria needs to be met before a product is considered to be done.

Done Done

- This means the product is coded, tested, defect-free, and accepted by the product owner.
- Hard commitment
- Once the team finishes their analysis, they make a hard commitment to a specific set of features to be delivered at the end of the iteration to the product owner.

Hardening iteration

- No new work is done during this iteration. In a hardening iteration, the team stops focusing on delivering new features and instead spends its time on stabilizing the system and getting it ready to be released.

Ideal time

- The time required to complete an activity assuming there are no interruptions so that work can be completed 100% efficiently.

Impediment

- An obstacle, situation, or event blocking the progress of a project during an iteration.

Iteration

Generally, an iteration is 2 to 4 weeks. Within the iteration, the team commits to develop a specific product, and at the same time, the product owner commits not to change the priorities within the iteration.

Iteration 0

- An Iteration Zero is an iteration where you set up all the servers, make sure we have a release plan, develop a product backlog, and in general do all those things that your project is ready to start.

Iteration backlog

- Prioritized user stories in the product backlog that the team is committed to developing during a particular iteration. The team is responsible for the iteration backlog. Items selected from the product backlog for the particular iteration.

Kaizen

- The Japanese management philosophy of continuous improvement.

Kanban

- Kanban means Signal. The team should update the Kanban board as the work progresses on the project. Kanban is a process designed to help teams work together more effectively. It is based on 3 basic principles

1. Visualize the workflow
2. Limit the amount of work in progress
3. Enhance the workflow

Participatory decision making

- The decision model where agile team members make decisions collaboratively and take ownership of the decision. The decision model is known as participatory decision making.

Product backlog

- The tool which represents the work remaining on the project is called a product backlog. It is the list of features developed in an iteration. It should be detailed, estimable, emergent, prioritized.

Product demo

- A customer review is called a product demo. It occurs on the last day of the iteration. The purpose of the meeting is for the team to show the customers and stakeholders the work they have done for the current iteration. The meeting is facilitated by the product owner.

Product owner

- The person is responsible to write user stories. They serve as a connection between the product owner and the team. Voice of the customer and representing stakeholders and business and setting priorities and deliverables.

Progressive elaboration

- It is a process of refining the product vision so that the high priority features are developed.

Reciprocal commitment

- The team commits to complete the user stories agreed in the iteration backlog, and the product owner is not changing the priorities during the iteration.

Refactoring

- Restructuring the code, without changing the external behavior.

Relative sizing

- Agile team orders stories on the wall in order of effort from the greatest to the least.

Release backlog

- The goal of the release is to deliver the subset of the product backlog called release backlog. After identifying which user stories will go into a particular release, the user stories become part of a release backlog.

Retrospective meeting

- The activity that a team reviews its performance to improve its performance. Held at the end of every iteration. Process centric meeting. During the retrospective, the team reflects on what happened in the iteration and identifies actions for improvement going forward.

Risk-adjusted backlog

- Defines feature priorities, taking into consideration of regulatory requirements. A risk-adjusted backlog takes into consideration the amount of risk a feature or user story places on the overall project.

Risk burn down chart

- A short period of the proof-of-concept of work is called a risk-based spike. It is used to explore the unknown. It displays how the total risk value changes over time. This chart used to manage project risks, by keeping us informed.

Scrum

- 3 pillars of scrum are Visibility, inspection, adoption. It is a framework that uses iterative cycles and incremental deliverables to develop solutions.

Self-organizing teams:

- The best architectures, requirements, and designs emerge from self-organizing teams.

Servant leadership

- -shield team from interruptions.
- -remove impediments that are blocking the progress of the project.
- -communicate project vision to the team.

Soft commitment

- The team makes a soft commitment to a specific set of features for the iteration backlog.

Shuffle time

- Time is taken to shift between activities during meetings. This time is not productive.

Sprint

Time boxed iteration of one month or less to build a potentially shippable product. Each sprint has

- Sprint planning
- Daily scrum
- development work
- Sprint review meeting
- Sprint retrospective meeting.

Sprint 0

- Focus on developing initial requirements, initial architecture, and setting up the environment, etc. A preliminary sprint exclusively dedicated to preparing for the first sprint.

Story map

- A way to organize user stories. A user story map arranges user stories into a useful model to help understand the functionality of the system.

Story point

- Fixed unit of development effort. Used to quantify the work effort and complexity required to develop a user story related to other stories.

Technical Dept.

- Technical decisions that a team chooses not to implement at this time, but will become obstacles if not done eventually. A team implementing some code as a quick fix, which is not following the organization standard, which would be a technical dept.

Time box

- Work cannot take more than the maximum amount of time defined. Time box within which work will be completed. E.g. Sprint Planning meeting time-boxed for 4 hours.

User story

- A user story is one or more sentences in the everyday business language of the end-user that captures what a user does as part of their job function.

Attributes of a user story

- INVEST (independent, negotiable, valuable, estimable, small, and testable).

Velocity

- The number of stories that a team can deliver within the iteration.

PMI-ACP® (AGILE CERTIFIED PRACTITIONER) PRACTICE EXAMS:

1. Which of the below choice is correct about continuous integration?

A. The code changes are checked into version control after every iteration.

B. The code changes are checked in for every release.

C. The code changes are checked in and tested every day.

D. The code changes are checked in once the project is complete.

2. Wireframe models used to help the agile teams with

A. It helps to elicit requirements that regular personas might miss.

B. A fictional user of the system under development

C. Confirm the created design.

D. None of the above.

3. One of the below is the valid list of emotional intelligence quadrants,

A. None of the below.

B. Forming, Storming, Norming, Performing.

C. Self, Others, Recognize, Regulate.

D. Self, Others, Regulate, Recognize.

4. One of the choices given below denotes dysfunctions of a team

A. Absence of trust.

B. Inattention to results.

C. Lack of commitment.

D. All of the above.

5. List the steps used in the estimating process,

A. Determine the size of the project. `

B. Calculate the work effort to do the work.

C. Convert the work effort into the schedule.

D. All of the above.

6. In the current iteration, the agile team committed for 20 story points. But during the last day of the iteration looks like they have completed only 15 story points. As an agile manager, what is your reaction?

A. Ignore the situation.

B. Complete the 15 story points and keep the remaining five story points in the backlog.

C. Cancel the current iteration.

D. Extend the iteration duration.

7. One of the following is correct about progressive elaboration,

A. Detailed planning occurs at the beginning.

B. No planning in progressive elaboration.

C. Detailed plan occurs as more details emerge in the project.

D. None of the above.

8. One of the options given below is the common failure modes,

A. Prefer to fail conservatively.

B. Making mistakes.

C. Being inconsistent.

D. All of the above.

9. A short period of proof-of-concept work is called as,

A. Risk-based-spike.

B. User story.

C. TDD (Test-driven development).

D. None of the above.

10. One of the benefits of retrospectives for the agile team,

A. Improved productivity

B. Improved quality.

C. Improved capacity.

D. All of the above.

11. One of the activities to help to set the stage in the retrospective process is,

A. Focus on/Focus off

B. ESVP

C. Check-in

D. All of the above.

12. In ESVP (Explorers, Shoppers, Vacationers, Prisoners), the definition of Vacationers is defined as,

A. They are eager to discover new ideas and insights.

B. They find all the available information & have a new idea based on that.

C. Vacationers are not interested in the retrospective work, to get away from the regular job they participate in the retrospective session.

D. They feel like they are forced to attend the retrospective session.

13. Lessons learnt happens during,

A. During only the first few iterations.

B. During the product demo.

C. Throughout the project duration.

D. Only after the project failure during the post review session.

14. Agile project teams do the planning at three levels named as,

A. Schedule, cost, quality

B. Release, iteration, retrospective.

C. Release, Iteration, Daily.

D. None of the above.

15. One of the following is a central repository that helps to track changes and save changes and provides the history of changes.

A. Release plan.

B. Product vision box.

C. Version control system.

D. None of the above.

16. The total number of story points planned for a release is called,

A. None of the below.

B. Release baseline.

C. Schedule baseline.

D. Performance measurement baseline

17. The main reason for most of the product failures are,

A. Technical risk.

B. Inefficient quality control.

C. Market risk.

D. None of the above.

18. The Waterfall approach is called as, and agile approach is called as,

A. Active, Reactive.

B. Not flexible, Flexible.

C. Plan driven, Value-driven.

D. All of the above.

19. When it is necessary to split a user story

A. Whenever the project manager thinks to split the story.

B. Not necessary to split the user story.

C. The user story is large to fit within a single iteration.

D. All of the above.

20. The agile triangle constraints are,

A. Time, Cost, Scope

B. Value, Quality, Constraint

C. Both of the above.

D. Both A and B are wrong

21. The process to minimize the work-in-process and maximize the business value is called,

A. XP

B. ITIL

C. None of the above.

D. Lean

22. The list of capabilities, stories, features that the product team identified is called,

A. Backlog.

B. User stories.

C. Capacity.

D. All of the above.

23. The usage of story cards in agile,

A. provides info about who is working in the team.

B. Both C and D.

C. It provides estimates about the stories.

D. It provides basic information about stories.

24. The least preferred contract type of agile project is,

A. Time & Materials Contract

B. Phased contract.

C. Agile iteration contract.

D. Firm Fixed Price Contract.

25. Remove obstacles for the team is the responsibility of scrum master. By removing obstacles, we are eliminating

A. Roadblocks.

B. Impediments.

C. Project Risk.

D. None of the above.

26. Risk mitigation technique that happens due to continuously integrate the code changes and confirm the changes to the code has not broken the base code is called,

A. None of the below.

B. Pair programming.

C. Continuous migration.

D. Continuous integration.

27. The diagram which reduces risk due to workload imbalance by spreading it more evenly is called as,

A. Pareto chart.

B. Burn up chart.

C. Cumulative Flow diagram.

D. Burn down chart.

28. A meeting which is for the team and by the team, in which the team choose the topic to discuss is called as,

A. Iteration planning meeting.

B. Open space meeting.

C. Retrospective meeting.

D. Daily standup meeting.

29. A typical, regular workday is called,

A. All of the below.

B. Ideal Day.

C. Normal Day.

D. Actual Day.

30. The day which is defined as the time required to complete an activity, assuming there are no interruptions so that work can be completed 100% efficiently,

A. Ideal days.

B. A & D

C. Actual Days.

D. Normal working day.

31. The time-boxed plan is what?

A. The product scope is committed, but the release date is not confirmed.

B. Both the product scope and release date approved in advance.

C. The release date is committed, but the features to be developed for the release is not defined.

D. None of the above.

32. When the agile team considers the factors that will support or oppose a change in the organization process is called,

A. Force field analysis.

B. Maslow's hierarchy of needs.

C. Deming PDCA cycle.

D. SWOT analysis.

33. The terminology in agile, which look forward in the future and learn the unknown and reduce the uncertainty is called,

A. Estimating.

B. Predicting.

C. Planning

D. Scanning.

34. Decisions are made at the time of last responsible moment is called

A. Project Commitment.

B. Deferring commitment.

C. Soft commitment.

D. Hard commitment.

35. To deliver the most valuable requirements to the customer first, makes the customer happy because they start realizing the benefits. This kind of product delivery is called

A. Rapid delivery.

B. Fast delivery.

C. None of the options A, B, D.

D. Incremental delivery.

36. If the defects are found very late in the agile software project, it causes

A. Less expensive.

B. More expensive.

C. It is not making any difference in cost.

D. cost savings.

37. Sam is working on the agile project and involved in developing software. The team is behind schedule. The software developed is not done thoroughly,

A. If it has bugs.

B. the software can't ship.

C. If the testing is not done.

D. the software can ship to the vendor.

38. In Agile EVM (Earned Value Measurement) the progress is usually measured at the end of

A. All of the below.

B. Project level.

C. Release level.

D. Iteration level.

39. Restructuring the code, without changing the external behavior of the code is called,

A. Working in pairs.

B. Validating the code.

C. Refactoring

D. bug fixing

40. Work in progress limit is defined as 10. The maximum number of things that can be allowed in the stream is,

A.11

B. 15

C. 10

D. 20

41. In Burn down charts, X and Y axis we track,

A. X-axis track time, and Y-axis track the work remaining

B. X-axis track the work remaining, and Y-axis track the time.

C. Both A & B.

D. None of the above.

42. The different levels of agile project planning are,

A. Project Vision.

B. Product Roadmap.

C. Release Planning.

D. All of the above.

43. The values used in agile modeling are,

A. Communication.

B. Simplicity.

C. Courage.

D. All of the above.

44. Prototyping is one of the agile,

A. Version control technique.

B. Feedback technique.

C. Code review.

D. code refactor method

45. The process which is performed frequently for the quality of the product is called,

A. Validation.

B. Frequent verification and validation.

C. Verification.

D. Inspection

46. Critical soft skills needed for any type of project,

A. Listening.

B. Negotiation.

C. Facilitation.

D. All of the above.

47. The agile manifesto, which is considered as team empowerment

A. Individuals and interactions over process and tools.

B. Working software over comprehensive documentation.

C. Customer collaboration over contract negotiation.

D. Responding to Change over following a plan.

48. An initial node in a large user story is called as

A. Epic

B.iteration log

C. User stories.

D. Task.

49. Self-organizing teams can make their own

A. The Product owner decides on a self-organizing team.

B. Scrum master decides on the self-organizing team.

C. Can't make their own decisions.

D. Decisions.

50. Project charter includes,

A. Milestones.

B. Critical success factors.

C. Vision.

D. All of the above.

PMI-ACP® (AGILE CERTIFIED PRACTITIONER) PRACTICE EXAM ANSWERS:

1. Answer: C Explanation: Option C is the correct answer. One risk mitigation technique used in an agile environment that developers need to continuously integrate their code to verify recent changes haven't broken the base code, which is already developed. Continuous Integration helps to find code issues as soon as possible.

2. Answer: C Explanation: Wireframes are simplified block diagrams that show the placement of elements in a user interface and demonstrate the intended layout and functionality of a solution. Option C is the correct answer. Option A is for Extreme persona. Option B is defined for Persona.

3. Answer: D Explanation: Option D is the correct answer. Option B is for the team formation stages. Option C is not correct.

4. Answer: D Explanation: Option D is the correct answer. The main dysfunctions of the agile team are the absence of trust, inattention to results, lack of commitment, fear of conflict, and avoidance of accountability.

5. Answer: D Explanation: Option D is the correct answer. The typical steps used in estimating process are determining the size of the project, calculate the work effort to do the work in hours, convert the work effort into the schedule, and calculate the cost.

6. Answer: B Explanation: Option B is the correct answer. Iteration is always time-boxed, and duration should not be extended. In this situation, the team should complete the 15 story points and keep the remaining 5 points in the backlog.

7. Answer: C Explanation: progressive elaboration is a process of refining the product vision so that the highest priority features are developed. In this planning occurs in phases rather than all at the beginning. Plan at high level in the beginning and detailed planning occurs close to the project.

8. Answer: D Explanation: Option D is the correct answer. The common failure modes are making mistakes, being inconsistent, being creatures of habit, prefer to fail conservatively.

9. Answer: A Explanation: Option A is the correct answer. A short period of a proof-of-concept of work is called risk-based-spike. Option B and Option D are not right.

10. Answer: D Explanation: Option D is the correct answer. The benefits of retrospectives of the agile team are improved productivity, improved quality, improved capacity, and improved capability.

11. Answer: D Explanation: Option D is the correct answer. In the Retrospective process the activities, help to set the stage is Focus on / Focus off, ESVP, working agreements, and check-in.

12. Answer: C Explanation: Option C is the correct answer for vacationers. Option A is for Explorers. Option B is for shoppers. Option D is for Prisoners.

13. Answer: C Explanation: Option C is the correct answer. Lessons learnt should be captured throughout the project from the team. If something good or bad happens during the project, the team remembers when it is fresh, and forget critical details after some time.

14. Answer: C Explanation: Option C is the correct answer. Three levels of planning are release, iteration, and daily. Other options A, B, and D are not correct.

15. Answer: C Explanation: The Version control system is a central repository that helps to track changes and save changes and provides the history of changes. Other options are not correct.

16. Answer: D Explanation: Performance measurement baseline is defined as the total number of story points planned for a release. Other options are not correct.

17. Answer: C. Explanation: The reason for product failure is market risk. None of the reasons given insignificant compared to market risk.

18. Answer: C. Explanation: In the waterfall (traditional) approach, everything is planned. It is called a Plan driven approach. An agile approach to the most valuable requirements to the customer are delivered; first, it is called value-driven approach. Other given options are not correct.

19. Answer: C Explanation: Sometimes, the user story is too large to fit into a single iteration. At those times, we need to split the user story.

20. Answer: B Explanation: Agile triangle relates to value, quality, and constraint. Time, Cost, Scope is related to traditional management.

21. Answer: D. Explanation: Value stream mapping is a lean tool used to analyze the value stream by means of eliminating waste, and minimize the work-in-process and maximize the value.

22. Answer: A. Explanation: The list of capabilities, stories, features that the product team identified is

called a backlog. It used to be maintained by the team, led/prioritized by the product owner.

23. Answer: D. Explanation: Story cards are used to provide necessary information about user stories like requirements, acceptance criteria, etc. Acceptance criteria are written on the back of the story card.

24. Answer: D. Explanation: Firm fixed-price contract is the least preferred contract type of agile projects. In this contract, the price is fixed, but agile welcome changes even at the last minute also. So it is difficult to accommodate changes in this type of contract.

25. Answer: C Explanation: By the way, removing obstacles/impediments, we are eliminating the risk of the agile project.

26. Answer: D Explanation: Continuous integration is one of the risk mitigation techniques used in an agile environment that developers need to continuously integrate their code to verify recent changes haven't broken the base code, which is already developed.

27. Answer: C Explanation: CFD, reduces risk due to workload imbalance by spreading it more evenly. This chart gives a quick overview of what is going in the project. We can find how much work is done, ongoing work, unfinished work, etc. It is used where the bottlenecks are there in the workflow. Through CFD, we can track how long it will take to deliver the desired

results, the total size of the backlog is reduced or constant or increasing.

28. Answer: B Explanation: The meeting, which is for the team and by the team, in which the team chooses the topic to discuss, is called an open space meeting.

29. Answer: D Explanation: A regular workday is called actual day, which starts at either 9 am or 8 am, and contains eight work hours and 1-hour break.

30. Answer: A. Explanation: Time required to complete an activity, assuming there are no interruptions so that work can be completed 100% efficiently is called ideal days.

31. Answer: C Explanation: In a time boxed plan, the release date is committed, but the features to be developed for the release are not defined.

32. Answer: A Explanation: Force field analysis is a tool used to examine organizational factors that are supporting or opposing the change. It considers the organization's driving and restraining forces.

33. Answer: D. Explanation: The terminology, which looks forward in the future and learns the unknown and reduce the uncertainty, is called scanning. Other options are not correct.

34. Answer: B Explanation: Decisions are made at the time of the last responsible moment is called Deferring commitment. Other options are not correct.

35. Answer: D. Explanation: Build the smallest thing possible to get value as soon as possible to the customer. E.g.: Release the software in incremental by releasing the key features in the first iteration.

36. Answer: B. Explanation: If we find the defects very late in the project, it is more expensive to fix it. If we find the errors very early in the project phase, it is less costly to fix.

37. Answer: B. Explanation: The developed software is not done completely, if the developed software cannot be shipped.

38. Answer: D Explanation: In Agile EVM, the progress is usually measured at the end of every iteration.

39. Answer: C Explanation: Restructuring the code, without changing the external behavior is called refactoring.

40. Answer: C Explanation: If the WIP limit is defined means, we can't add more than the limit to the value stream.

41. Answer: A Explanation: In burn down chart plotted against the time vs work remaining. In x axis, we plot the time and the Y-axis; we plot the work remaining in the project.

42. Answer: D. Explanation: The different levels of agile project planning are product vision, product roadmap, release planning, and iteration planning, daily stand-up.

43. Answer: D. Explanation: The four values used in agile modeling are communication, simplicity, courage, and feedback.

44. Answer: B Explanation: Prototype is used to get valuable feedback from the users early in the project.

45. Answer: B. Explanation: The process which is performed frequently for the quality of the product is called frequent verification and validation.

46. Answer: D Explanation: Critical soft skills are listening, negotiation, conflict resolution, facilitation.

47. Answer: A. Explanation: Individuals and interactions over process and tools, this manifesto is related to team empowerment.

48. Answer: A. Explanation: Epic span around many iterations called a capacity. It is the largest part of the

user story. Epic is a larger user story, can be decomposed into smaller user stories.

49. Answer: D Explanation: Self-organizing team can make their own decisions. The best architectures, requirements, and designs emerge from self-organizing teams.

50. Answer: D. Explanation: Project charter includes project vision, milestones, and critical success factors.

Scenario based PMP Practice Questions: (50 Questions)

1. Select the characteristic related to the project from the choices given below.

A. A project can create a service or capability to perform a service.

B. It has a definite beginning and an end.

C. A project is a temporary endeavor undertaken to create a unique product.

D. All of the above.

2. Max is working in a matrix organization. Sam has worked for a couple of years in a functional organization. Now both Max and Sam are working

together on a project. During their discussion, Sam has an argument with Max regarding one of the project constraints that he mentioned. As per Sam one of the choices given below is not a valid project constraint, which is?

A. Risk.

B. Market demand.

C. Quality.

D. Budget.

3. Chris is the project manager for an agile project, and the project is going to be completed in another 3 months. Already the project cost overrun and it is behind the schedule. Since it is one of the key stakeholder's interest, the project team is continuing the project. One of the given options is not valid for project trigger, which is?

A. Project manager's wish.

B. Customer request.

C. Technological advance.

D. Market demand.

4. Carl is assigned as a project manager by the PMO of the organization. Rick is the operations manager of the product that Carl's team is delivering. The team is aware of the fact that both the operations work and

the project work is different. One of the below options is considered as an operational work, identify it.

A. Has a definite start period and end period.

B. Work is repeatable and ongoing.

C. Creates a unique product.

D. Progressively elaborated.

5. David is working in the supportive PMO structure and responsible for the project as well as provides support functions to the project. Randy is working as a project manager in his team. Sam also reports to David, and handles a group of projects in a program. How can they distinguish between project, program and portfolio management?

A. A project is a collection of related projects which are closely linked, Program is a temporary endeavor undertaken to create a unique product, and Portfolio is a group of projects or programs which are linked together by a common objective.

B. A portfolio is a collection of related projects which are closely linked, Project is a temporary endeavor undertaken to create a unique product, and Program is a group of projects or programs which are linked together by a common objective.

C. A program is a collection of related projects which are closely linked, Project is a temporary endeavor undertaken to create a unique product, and Portfolio is a group of projects or programs which are linked together by a common objective.

D. A Portfolio is a collection of related projects which are closely linked, Program is a temporary endeavor undertaken to create a unique product, and Project is a group of projects or programs which are linked together by a common objective.

6. Sam is working in a company's PMO. One of the below objectives is not related to the PMO objective. Which one is it?

A. Manage the project.

B. Manage shared resources.

C. Coaching, mentoring and providing guidance.

D. Identify and develop project management methodology, standards and best practices.

7. Ralph is working as a project manager in a tight schedule project. He is using the crashing/fast-tracking to compress the schedule to finish the project on time. Ralph is reporting to a PMO structure in which the level of control is high, moderate and low. Identify the PMO structure that Ralph is reporting to.

A. Directing, supportive and controlling.

B. Directing, controlling and supportive.

C. Supportive, Directing and controlling.

D. Controlling, Supportive and directive.

8. Smith is the Project manager who deals with the project management strategy and project team in a critical project for the organization. He is working in a strong matrix organization and supported by a directive PMO structure. One of the below is not the core competencies of the project manager, identify it.

A. Performance.

B. Personal.

C. Conflict management.

D. Knowledge.

9. Michael is working as a director, and reports to the PMO who manages all the projects, shares the resources in between projects, provides methods, tools and techniques, and guidance. PMO can take key decisions related to the project such as terminate or postpone the project. Robert is working as a project manager and reports to the PMO structure which provides polices and guidelines. Such a structure is known as?

A. Controlling.

B. Directing.

C. Supportive.

D. None of the above.

10. Karen is working in a startup organization. He was appointed by the PMO. The PMO structure which appoints project managers and manages all the projects in his organization is known as?

A. Controlling.

B. Directing.

C. Supportive.

D. None of the above.

11. Ken is the project manager in a cloud project, which migrates all the software code to the cloud. In his organization project manager shares the authority with the functional manager. Lisa is the functional manager in the same organization, working for a long time. Lisa and Ken are working on the project which has a tight budget. One of the matrix organization in the below options is not a valid matrix organization. Identify the wrong one.

A. Strong matrix organization.

B. Balanced matrix organization.

C. Project matrix organization.

D. Weak matrix organization.

12. Richard is working in an organization as a project manager in which the project manager does the administrative tasks, doesn't have much power and reports to the functional manager. Identify the type of organization that Richard works for.

A. Matrix organization.

B. Projectized organization.

C. Functional organization.

D. Weak matrix organization.

13. Paul is working in an organization in which the project manager has the most authority and responsible for the project's success and they can take important decisions regarding budget, schedule, and resources in the project. Identify the type of organization in which Paul works for.

A. Matrix organization.

B. Projectized organization.

C. Functional organization.

D. Weak matrix organization.

14. Sam is working in an organization in which the project manager's role is part-time and decisions are taken by the functional manager, their role is similar

to that of project expeditor. Identify the type of organization in which Sam works for.

A. Matrix organization.

B. Functional organization.

C. Strong matrix organization.

D. Weak matrix organization.

15. Paul is the project manager in a technology company which innovates smart technology projects. He used to conduct daily stand up meetings at 9 am. His offshore team members and onsite team members participate in the daily stand-up meetings. In today's meeting, they had an argument related to risks. One of the team members argues that only the initiating stage risks are higher, and in the later stages, risks will be reduced. During which phase of the project are risks and uncertainties higher?

A. Planning.

B. Executing.

C. Initiating.

D. Monitor & control.

16. Will and Ted are working in an organization in which project managers and functional managers work together to complete the project work. Identify

the type of organization in which Project expeditors and coordinators don't exist.

A. Functional.

B. Projectized.

C. Strong matrix.

D. Weak matrix.

17. Joy is the tech lead in the organization which manufactures LCD TVs. He reports to Pamela, and she reports to the directive PMO structure. Their organization is going to start a new project soon. Pamela asked Joy to identify the stakeholders impacted by the project. Joy is reviewing one of the below documents used to identify people who are affected by the project. Identify the document.

A. Project plan.

B. Risk register.

C. Stakeholder register.

D.WBS.

18. A project can be divided into any number of phases. A phase is a collection of logically related activities in order to complete one or more deliverables. Project phases can be sequential or overlap, and it depends on the situation. A Project is separated into different logical groups which are

called phases for the purpose of management, planning and control. The number of phases in the project depends on the size, complexity and impact of the project. Every phase needs to go through all the 5 process groups. During closing of the phase the product can be handed over to the customers for review, and based on the feedback, the next phase starts. Most of the projects have the below types of phase-to-phase relationship. One of the given below is not a valid phase-to-phase relationship. Which one is it?

A. Overlapping relationship.

B. Sequential relationship.

C. Iterative relationship.

D. Parallel relationship.

19. Taylor and Crystal are working in a strong matrix organization. Crystal is a functional manager and represents the assembly line. One of the projects they are working together on has a phase-to-phase relationship, the next phase starts only if the previous phase is complete. Identify the correct relationship below.

A. Overlapping relationship.

B. Sequential relationship.

C. Iterative relationship.

D. None of the above.

20. Wilson is a team member and working in a project which has zero-tolerance related to scope, schedule and cost. He is reporting directly to David, who is the functional manager. David asked Wilson to identify the enterprise environmental factors available in the project. One of the below is not a valid EEF (enterprise environmental factor). Identify the wrong option given below.

A. Market condition.

B. Lessons learned databases.

C. Government and industry standards.

D. Organizational culture, structure and governance.

21. Kevin is recently promoted to a project manager position, and he is reporting to directive PMO structure. John is managing the PMO, and he follows directive PMO structure. John asked Kevin to review the corporate knowledge base to identify the project constraints for a similar project that Kevin is going to start. Kevin found out that one of the below is not a valid OPA (organizational process asset). Identify it.

A. Lessons learned databases.

B. Project records, files from previous projects.

C. Market condition.

D. Templates, guidelines, and procurement policies.

22. Sara and Tim are working on a project which is done by multiple iterations. They are working in the last iteration, after which the product will be handed over to the customer in a week after sign-off. They are not sure what kind of task they are going to be assigned to after this project from the organization. Identify this type of organization structure, in which when the project is complete the team members don't have any place (no home) to back and continue the work.

A. Projectized.

B. Functional.

C. Strong matrix.

D. Weak matrix.

23. William is the project manager and has a team of 7 members, they are working in project delivery which has short iterations. Sam is working as a functional manager. William and Sam are working together on the current project. Team members are sometimes confused about whom to report to when there is an issue or escalation. Identify this type of organization structure in which conflicts are more, and resource

allocation is difficult also the team members have more than one person to report to.

A. Functional.

B. Projectized.

C. Matrix.

D. None of the above.

24. Dorothy is working in an organization in which duties are grouped by specialty. John is the project manager, but he is not having influence/power in the project. He is working as an assistant to Dorothy. John is doing mostly administrative tasks in the project. Identify this type of organization structure in which resources are grouped based on specialty and the project manager has less authority.

A. Projectized.

B. Strong matrix organization.

C. Weak matrix organization.

D. Functional organization.

25. Requirements from the customer are prioritized in backlog and work is done by taking the high priority item in the backlog, it is known as a predictive lifecycle. In this lifecycle scope, cost and schedule are determined in the early stage of the project, before

starting the work. Predictive lifecycle is also known as?

A. Adaptive lifecycle.

B. Plan driven lifecycle.

C. Iterative lifecycle.

D. Change driven lifecycle.

26. Smith is working as a project manager in an organization known as Firstcorp. He follows all the 5 process group initiating of planning, executing, monitor and control and closing to complete the project. Currently, he is working on developing project charter as well as identifying the stakeholders in the project. The process group which identifies the stakeholders as well as develop project charter is called?

A. Planning.

B. Monitor and control.

C. Initiating.

D. Closing.

27. Peter is working in a plan-driven project work. He is involved in the process of developing a project document that formally gives him authority over the project to assign resources required to complete the project. This process is known as?

A. Planning.

B. Monitor and control.

C. Project charter.

D. Closing.

28. Maria is working as a developer in a software development project. Since her manager got a promotion, they moved her to the manager's position. And she is new to the role assigned to her. She is actively involved in executing the project as per defined in the project management plan. Smith is her director, and he asked her which stage of the project she is working on? What is Maria's answer to her director from the given choices?

A. Planning.

B. Monitor and control.

C. Initiating.

D. Direct and manage project work.

29. Andrew is the project manager in an iterative project. He is closely working with the change control board, for changes in the project. Mostly Andrew works in a process which measures and monitors the progress and performance of the project, and identifies if there are any variances and take corrective actions if needed. This process is known as?

A. Planning.

B. Monitor and control project work.

C. Initiating.

D. Executing.

30. The knowledge area which includes the processes and activities to identify, define, combine and coordinate the various processes and project management activities within the project management process groups is called?

A. stakeholder management.

B. Integration management.

C. Quality management.

D. Communications management.

31. Fred is working on the process that the main output is the final product, final report and project document updates. Identify the process group that Fred is currently involved with.

A. Direct and manage project work.

B. Develop project charter.

C. Monitor and control project work.

D. Closing.

32. Joe is assigned as a project manager for an innovative project, which creates bots. Joe plans the Work to be done in the near (next) iteration is planned in detail, and the work in the future is planned at a higher level. After the customer reviewed the work, and updates are done in the product, the next iteration is planned in detail. Planning is an iterative process, and it must be done throughout the project as more information is available. This act is known as?

A. Continuous iteration.

B. Iteration planning.

C. Progressive elaboration.

D. None of the above.

33. Keith is the project manager in a time-sensitive project. The leadership style in the project allows team members to make their own decisions and establish their own goals. Identify the leadership style in the organization that Keith is working in.

A. Servant leader.

B. Transactional.

C. Laissez-faire.

D. Transformational.

34. Rita is working as a team member in a pharmaceutical company that develops medicines for rare diseases. And she is working in the EDI division (electronic data interchange) to automate the transactions. She is reporting to Mary who is the project manager and many in the office like her characteristics and personality. Some of the effective characteristics that a project manager should have to be successful are?

A. Courteous, creative.

B. Emotional, intellectual.

C. Political, service-oriented.

D. All of the above.

35. Dalia is working as a Director of the organization. Michael is reporting to Dalia, and he is having excellent project management skills. The project got approved, and it is progressing by iterations. Michael's duties in this process group are; measure progress and performance, find out the variance, and recommend preventive and corrective actions through change control and provide updates to the project management plan. This process is known as?

A. Manage project knowledge.

B. Develop project management plan.

C. Monitor and control project work.

D. Develop project charter.

36. ABC Corporation is the market leader in manufacturing industry. James is working on an agile project which has multiple iterations. His main duties as defined in the project management plan is to implement approved changes to achieve the project objectives. What are the main outputs of the process group James is involved in?

A. Project charter, Assumption log.

B. Final product, Final report.

C. Deliverables, Change requests, issue log.

D. All of the above.

37. Ronald is working on a complex project, which he needs to work with the functional managers. Currently, he is involved in the process group which obtains formal sign-off from customer for the project or phase, measure customer satisfaction, archive project records and documents, document lessons learned and release the resources. The process which Ronald is involved in is called?

A. Direct and manage project work.

B. monitor and control project work.

C. Close project.

D. Perform integrated change control.

38. Pyramid Corporation is involved in manufacturing car spare parts for the past 20 years. They are the market leaders in the segment. Mathew is working as an IT manager for Pyramid Corporation. Mathew is recoding the conflicts, gaps, issues in the issue log, which help him effectively track and manage issues and to ensure it is resolved in a timely manner. He is updating the issue log in the monitor and control activities process during the project. The data on the issue log contains?

A. Final solution, priority.

B. Issue type, who is assigned to the issue.

C. Status, who raised the issue.

D. All of the above.

39. In general project management process, groups are placed into the below categories. Which process group needs to be included in all the projects?

A. Initiating, planning, executing.

B. Initiating, planning, executing, monitor and control, closing.

C. Initiating, planning, executing, monitor and control.

D. Initiating, planning, monitor and control and closing.

40. Edward is the program manager in a sports goods manufacturing company. Ralph and Sam are reporting to Edward on a regular basis regarding the development of the project. Ralph and Sam are interacting with many other department project managers, and they are involved in other project-related meetings also. Ralph's project is part of the program, and the program has other critical projects also. The other projects in the program may impact Ralph's project due to below reason.

A. Priorities of the funding, Distribution of deliverables.

B. Demand for the same resource, Alignment of project goals and objectives related to the organization.

C. Both A and B.

D. Only B.

41. The project charter formally authorizes a project. Project charter authorizes the PM to apply resources to complete the work on the project. It is the first thing done in a project. An approved project charter initiates the project. One of the below options related to project charter is not correct. Identify the incorrect option.

A. Authorizes the PM to apply resources to complete the work on the project.

B. Documents the business needs, assumptions, constraints, risks, high-level requirements, etc.

C. It describes, that the project is worth the investment.

D. Formally authorize the project.

42. Joseph is working with PMO in one of the projects. He is an expert in all knowledge areas, and has a better view of the project. Integration management includes the processes and activities that coordinate various project management activities. One of the given processes is not related to project integration management, which is?

A. Develop project charter, develop project management plan.

B. Develop a business case.

C. Direct and manage project work, monitor and control project work.

D. Perform integrated change control, close project/phase.

43. Tech Systems is an innovative technology company using artificial intelligence in their reject project. They are making robots for some of the automation work. Charles is working as a project manager in this project and deals with resource

allocation, examining alternative project approaches, and managing the interdependencies in the project. One of the given options is not valid output in project integration management, identify which.

A. Project charter, Deliverables.

B. Project management plan, approved change requests.

C. Change requests, work performance report.

D. Scope management plan.

44. John is the senior project manager in a project and he spends most of his time with stakeholders for the funding approval. He is working on the input which describes the product scope description, the business need and how the project supports the strategic plan. This process that John is working on is called?

A. Business case.

B. Project charter.

C. Project statement of work.

D. Project management plan.

45. Configuration management is part of PMIS. Steve is the key stakeholder in the project, as well as he is managing the project. Steve is involved in some of the Configuration management activities performed in

the integrated change control process. In general these activities are known as?

A. Configuration identification.

B. Configuration status accounting.

C. Configuration verification and audit.

D. All of the above.

46. Business case is one of the key inputs to develop the project charter process in project integration management. Daniel is the project manager and trying to convince the project board to support it. He is preparing for the town hall meeting to explain the proposal that is worth the investment. During the process, he is creating the business case. Business case is created as a result of?

A. Organization need, market demand.

B. Legal requirement, Technological advancement.

C. Social need, customer request.

D. All of the above.

47. Information management tools and techniques are used to create and connect people to get information. Randy is working on some of the Information management tools in his project. Some of the tools and techniques related to information management are?

A. Lessons learned register.

B. PMIS (project management information systems).

C. library services, information gathering.

D. All of the above.

48. Christopher is the senior analyst in an agile project. He is involved in the process of reviewing the change requests by the board based on the merits and demerits, approve or reject them and manage the changes. This process is called?

A. Change control process.

B. Perform integrated change control process.

C. Change control board.

D. Change control meeting.

49. Scheduling tool, configuration management system, work authorization system all are part of PMIS. The formal documented procedure which describes how to authorize and initiate the work in the right sequence and the right time is known as?

A. Project management plan.

B. Project charter.

C. Work authorization system.

D. Organization chart.

50. Donald is the project manager in one of the projects, which is part of the program. He is working in project integration management and taking care of all the process in the integration management. In this phase of the project, he is mostly involved in directing and managing project work. One of the options given below is not a valid input to direct and manage the work process, which one is it?

A. Project management plan.

B. Business Case.

C. Approved change requests.

D. EEF (Enterprise Environmental Factor), OPA (Organizational process Asset).

Answers to PMP Practice Questions:

Note: EEF – Enterprise Environmental Factors, OPA – organizational Process Assets.

1. Answer: D. A project is a temporary endeavor undertaken to create a unique product. It has a definite beginning and an end. It can be a part of a program or portfolio. Project drive changes to the organization.

2. Answer. B. Market demand is not a valid project constraint. Valid project constraints are risk, quality, resources, budget, scope and schedule.

3. Answer: Option A is not a valid option for project trigger. Valid options are legal requirements, market demand, customer request, technology and social needs.

4. Answer: Option B is correct. Operations work is ongoing and repeatable. Other options are related to the characteristics of the project.

5. Answer: Option C is correct. Program is a collection of related projects which are closely linked, Project is a temporary endeavor undertaken to create a unique product, and Portfolio is a group of projects or programs which are linked together by a common objective.

6. Answer: Option A is not an objective of PMO. It is one of the project manager's tasks. The functions of PMO are;

- Manage shared resources.
- Coaching, mentoring, guidance whenever needed.
- Identify and develop project management methodology, standards and best practices.
- Monitoring compliance with project management processes by audits.
- Develop and manage organizational process assets such as procedures, templates, policies.
- Communications between projects.

7. Answer: Option B is correct. The level of control is high in directive PMO Structure. The level of control is medium in controlling PMO Structure. The level of control is low in supportive PMO structure.

8. Answer: Option C is not one of the core competencies of a project manager. It is one of the interpersonal skills of a project manager. Project managers should have the competencies shown below,

- Knowledge: How much they know about project management.
- Performance: A project manager is able to apply the knowledge to get the results.
- Personal: It is the attitude and other personal characteristics, leadership shown when doing the project.

9. Answer: Option A is correct. Based on the control and influence the PMO structure may be,

- **Supportive**: This type serves as a project repository, and the role in this type is consultative. The level of control is low.
- **Controlling**: It has a moderate level of control. Provide supportive roles and requires compliance.
- **Directing**: Directly involves in projects and programs. The level of control is high.

10. Answer: Option B is correct. Directing PMO structure which appoints project manager and manages all the projects in the organization.

11. Answer: Option B is not a valid matrix organization. Other options are correct. Matrix organization is subdivided into 3 categories as weak matrix organization, strong matrix organization and balanced matrix organization.

12. Answer: Option C is correct. Richard is working in a functional organization. In a Functional organization:

- Project team reports to functional managers.
- Organization is grouped by functional areas e.g.: marketing, sales etc.
- Project managers have not much influence/power in this type of organization.
- Project managers work as an assistant to the functional managers.
- Project managers mostly work on administrative tasks in the project.

13. Answer: Option B is correct. Paul is working in a projectized organization.

Projectized organization:

- Project teams are grouped based on the projects. Once the project work is done, the project team is disbanded and the team members continue to work on other projects.

- The project manager is responsible for the project's success and has authority.
- The project manager can make key decisions related to resources, budget, and schedule.
- Project coordinators and expeditors won't exist in projectized organization.
- When the work is complete, the team members don't have departments to go back to.

14. Answer: Option D is correct. Sam is working in a weak matrix organization.

Weak matrix organization:

- Functional manager has more authority than the project manager.
- Major project decisions are taken by the functional manager.
- Project manager role in this type of organization is part time.
- Power of project manager is similar to expeditor (can't make any decisions in the project) and project coordinators (can make some decisions).

15. Answer: Option C is correct. During the Initiating phase of the projects project risks and uncertainties are higher. Risk and uncertainty high at the beginning of

the project and decrease during the course of the project.

16. Answer: Option B is correct. In a projectized organization, Project expeditors and coordinators don't exist. In a weak matrix organization the Power of project manager is similar to expeditor (can't make any decisions in the project) and project coordinators (can make some decisions).

17. Answer: Option C is correct. Stakeholder register is used to identify the people who are affected by the project. A stakeholder register is used to identify the stakeholders involved in the project who can provide information related to the requirements. Also it contains the key requirements for the project.

18. Answer: Option D is not a valid phase-to-phase relationship. Valid phase-to-phase relationship is sequential relationship and overlapping relationship.

19. Answer: Option B is correct. Sequential phase-to-phase relationship, the next phase starts only if the previous phase is complete. This step-by-step approach reduces risk, but the overall schedule may be impacted.

20. Answer: Option B is OPA (organizational process asset). It refers to conditions that are not under the project team's control, and it influences the project.

Some of the EEF (Enterprise environmental factors) are:

- Market condition.
- Organizational culture, structure and governance.
- Human resources.
- Personal administration.
- Political conditions.
- Work authorization system.
- PMIS (project management information systems).
- Government and industry standards.
- Commercial databases.
- Stakeholder risk tolerance.
- Infrastructure.
- Communication channels.

21. Answer: Option C is EEF (Enterprise environmental factor). Some of the OPA are,

- Historical records.
- Templates.
- Plans, processes and procedures.
- Lessons learned.

22. Answer: Option A is correct. In a Projectized organization;

- Project teams are grouped based on the projects. Once the project work is done, the project team is disbanded and the team members continue to work on other projects.
- Project manager is responsible for the project's success and has authority.
- Project manager can make key decisions related to resources, budget, and schedule.
- Project coordinators and expeditors won't exist in projectized organization.
- When the work is complete, the team members don't have departments to go back.

23. Answer: Option C is correct. In a Matrix organization conflicts are more, and resource allocation is difficult also the team members have more than one person to report.

24. Answer: Option D is correct. Some of the characteristics of a functional organization are:

- Project team reports to functional managers.
- Organization is grouped by functional areas e.g.: marketing, sales, etc.
- Project managers have no much influence/power in this type of organization.
- They work as an assistant to the functional managers.

- Project managers mostly work on administrative tasks in the project.

25. Answer: Option B is correct. Predictive life cycle is also called plan-driven lifecycle. In this lifecycle scope, cost and schedule are determined in the early stage of the project, before starting the work. Projects go through series of sequential or overlapping phases. Project is initiated and the team define the scope of the project, then creates the plan to develop the product, and execute the work. Any changes to the scope are managed through the change control process and it requires re-planning and formal acceptance.

When the scope is well known then the project work is done by the predictive lifecycle.

26. Answer: Option C is correct. Initiating process is to define and authorization to start the project. Initiate the project and decide what is going to be built for the project. It is using the identify stakeholder and develop project charter. The main outputs in this process group are project charter, identified stakeholders and stakeholder register. Project manager is assigned during this process. Once the project charter is approved, the project starts officially.

27. Answer: Option C is correct. It formally authorizes a project. Project charter authorizes the PM to apply resources to complete the work on the project. It is the

first thing done on a project. An approved project charter initiates the project.

It is in the Initiating process group. Since project is sponsored by sponsors, charter needs to be approved by sponsors. PM should be allocated while developing the project charter for the purpose of understanding the requirements. Charter identifies the business needs and stakeholders' expectations.

28. Answer: Option D is correct. Executing process, executes the defined plan, to complete the work defined in project management plan. Actual project work is done in the executing process group. Project costs are usually high in this process group since it is utilizing all the resources to complete the project. As per the project management plan execution process group perform the activities to complete the work defined. It involves managing stakeholders and their expectations, manage resources, and perform the activities as per the project management plan.

During execution of project the plan may change, and the baselines must be updated to reflect the changes. As a result change requests are created to bring back the project as per the plan. Change request approvals are done for preventive, corrective actions and defect repairs.

29. Answer: Option B is correct. Monitor and control measures and monitors the progress and performance of the project, and identify if there are any variances and take corrective actions if needed.

30. Answer: Option B is correct. The knowledge area integrates with all parts of the project is called project integration management.

31. Answer: Option D is correct. Project enters into the closing process group when the project phase is completed or the project is completed. The closing process group formally completes all the activities across all project management groups in a project phase or a project or contractual obligations. Premature closure of the project is also formally done in this process group. During project closure, the following may happen.

- Obtain formal sign-off from customer for the project or phase.
- Conduct post-project review.
- Measure customer satisfaction.
- Archive project records and documents.
- Document lessons learned.
- Update organizational project assets.
- Transfer products to operations.
- Release the team.
- Close the contract.

32. Answer: Option C is correct. Planning is an iterative process, and it must be done throughout the project as more information is available is called progressive elaboration. Work to be done in the near (next) iteration is planned in detail, and the work in the future is planned at a higher level. It is called progressive elaboration.

33. Answer: Option C is correct.

Laissez-faire: Allows the team to make their own decisions and establish their own goals.

Charismatic: The leader has a high energy level and enthusiastic and self-confident. Able to inspire the team by their activities.

Servant leader: This type of leader committed to serve and put others first. They focus on other people's growth, learning, development, autonomy and well-being.

Interactional: This type of leader has the combination of transactional, transformational and charismatic leadership styles.

Transactional: This type of a leader focuses on goals, feedback and accomplishment to determine rewards.

Transformational: They empower the followers through encouragement for innovation and creativity and individual consideration.

34. Answer: Option D is correct. An effective project manager has the following characteristics.

- Courteous
- Creative
- Authentic
- Intellectual
- Managerial
- Political
- Social
- Service-oriented
- cultural

35. Answer: Option C is correct. The activities in the monitor and control process group are measure progress and performance, find out the variance, and recommend preventive and corrective actions through change control, updates to the project management plan.

Monitoring and control process group track, measure and review the progress and performance of the project, to ensure the project is on track and identify areas in which changes to the plan are required and initiate the changes. Performance is measured at regular intervals to verify the variance from the project management plan.

36. Answer: Option C is correct. James is working on the process to direct and manage project work. The key outputs of the process are:

- Deliverables,
- change requests,
- issue log,
- work performance data,
- project management plan updates,
- project document updates,
- OPA updates.

37. Answer: Option C is correct. The process group which Obtains formal sign-off from the customer for the project or phase, Measure customer satisfaction, Archive project records and documents, Document lessons learned, Release the team is called closing.

Project enters into the closing process group when the project phase is completed or the project is completed. The closing process group formally completes all the activities across all project management groups in a project phase or a project or contractual obligations. Premature closure of the project is also formally done in this process group. During project closure, the following may happen.

- Obtain formal sign-off from customer for the project or phase.
- Conduct post-project review.

- Measure customer satisfaction.
- Archive project records and documents.
- Document lessons learned.
- Update organizational project assets.
- Transfer products to operations.
- Release the team.
- Close the contract.

38. Answer: Option D is correct. This log keeps recording all the issues occurred during execution of the project, and it needs to be shared with the stakeholders. This log is kept updated throughout the project, whenever new issues are identified. An issue log is the project document, where all the issues are recorded and tracked, data on issue log includes;

- Issue type, who raised the issue and when, description, priority, who is assigned to the issue, target resolution date, status and final solution.

39. Answer: Option B is correct. Initiating, planning, executing, monitor and control, closing process groups must be included in all the projects.

40. Answer: Option C is correct. The projects within a program may impact a project due to.

- Priorities of funding.
- Demand for the same resource.

- Alignment of project goals and objectives with the organization.
- Distribution of deliverables.

41. Answer: Option C is not correct. It is related to business case.

Project charter formally authorizes a project. Project charter authorizes the PM to apply resources to complete the work on the project. It is the first thing done in a project. An approved project charter initiates the project.

It is in the Initiating process group. Since project is sponsored by sponsors, charter needs to be approved by sponsors. PM should be allocated while developing the project charter for the purpose of understanding the requirements. Charter identifies the business needs and stakeholders' expectations.

Key Contents of Project Charter:

- Project Title and description.
- Stakeholders.
- Business case.
- Project constraints and assumptions.
- Sponsor for the project.
- Stakeholder influence/authority level.
- Product description.
- Budget for the project.

- PM & their roles, authority etc.
- Project Risks.
- Project justification.

42. Answer: Option B is not a process in project integration management. Valid processes in project integration management are:

- Develop project charter.
- Develop project management plan.
- Direct and manage project work.
- Manage project knowledge.
- Monitor and control project work.
- Perform integrated change control.
- Close project or phase.

43. Answer: Option D is not a valid output. Valid outputs from project integration management are:

- Project charter.
- Project management plan.
- Assumption log, issue log.
- Deliverables, work performance data.
- Change requests, lessons learned register, work performance reports.
- Approved change requests, final product.
- Project document updates, OPA updates.

44. Answer: Option C is correct. Project statement of work describes the business need, the product scope description and how the project supports the strategic plan. It describes the product that is delivered by the project.

45. Answer: Option D is correct. The activities related to configuration management performed in perform integration management are configuration identification, configuration status accounting, configuration verification and audit.

46. Answer: Option D is correct. Business case is created as a result of:

- Market demand.
- Customer request.
- Organizational needs.
- Legal requirement.
- Technological advance.
- Social needs.
- Ecological impact.

47. Answer: Option D is correct. Information management tools and techniques are used to create and connect people to information. Some of the tools and techniques involved in information management are:

- Lessons learned register.

- Library services.
- PMIS.
- Information gathering.

48. Answer: Option B is correct. Perform integrated change control process reviewing the change requests by the board based on the merits and demerits approve or reject them, manage the changes.

49. Answer: Option C is correct. Work authorization system is used to manage when and what sequence the project work will be done. Scheduling tool, configuration management system, work authorization system all are part of PMIS.

50. Answer: Option B is not a valid input. Valid inputs to direct and manage work are:

- Project management plan.
- Project documents.
- Approved change requests.
- EEF.
- OPA.

Congratulations!

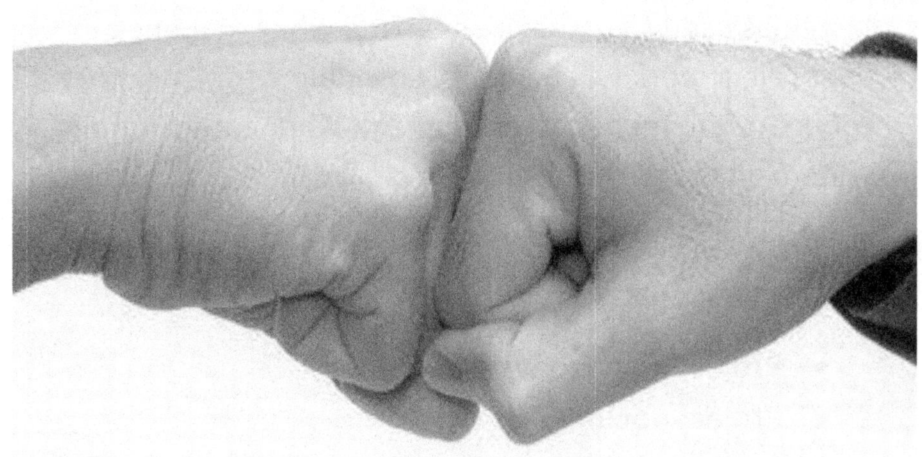

You did it!!!

Made in the USA
Coppell, TX
10 May 2023

16637347R00193